# the Stork

**Bar Book**

# Club

*by* Lucius Beebe

Martino Publishing
Mansfield Centre, CT
2015

*Martino Publishing*
*P.O. Box 373,*
*Mansfield Centre, CT 06250 USA*


ISBN 978-1-61427-817-7

Cover design by T. Matarazzo

*Printed in the United States of America On 100% Acid-Free Paper*

# the Stork

Bar Book

# Club

*by* Lucius Beebe

Rinehart & Company, Inc.

*New York* $\frac{19}{46}$ *Toronto*

# Contents:

Foreword: If there had never been a Stork Club, mankind in his vast and urgent necessity would have invented one. This is, to be sure, a corruption of an epigram evolved by a celebrated philosopher about man and his relationship with Divinity and not the profound reflection of the author of this handy manual to gulping and guzzling. But it is altogether and entirely true. The Stork and the man who created it are equally the product of their times and the personal and emotional complement to the essentially naive hanker on the part of the American public for snobbishness and glamour in Cecil de Mille proportions.

Gene Fowler once remarked: "The history of Greece is written in its temples, that of the United States in its hotels." And to carry the parallel even farther, a good deal of the history of New York has been written in its restaurants, saloons, night clubs, cafes, cabarets, bars, lounges, dining rooms, ordinaries, fish and chips, chophouses, dives, deadfalls, beer stubes, dramshops and all the allied institutions dedicated to the stoking and sluicing of customers of many tastes and means.

More than any other city on earth, New York lives in public. It drinks, dines and dances in multiple postures in public places and it takes inordinate pleasure in reading about itself so occupied and admiring photographs of itself tearing at Scotch grouse, hoisting schooners of beer or tossing clamshells on the sawdust floor as its pleasure may dictate. The by-products of public eating and drinking in themselves are a vast industry and preposterous salaries are paid quite ordinary newspaper reporters whose almost sole concern is with the inmates of the town's various plush and chromium cocktail zoos. Magazine and newspaper columns are regularly devoted to the business of food and drink on a truly heroic scale. It is probably the only metropolis since Imperial Rome where who eats what and with whom is top column news to millions.

The last four decades of New York's night life have been blazingly illuminated with names awash with gustatory and social glamour. Its saloons and cafes have become a glittering tradition and the mere names, Delmonico, Sherry, Ritz, Bustanoby, Rector and Shanley, have become synonymous with sumptuous doings and monster skirmishes among the wine cards.

In the current generation, when uninhibited public dining has raised the salaries of wine stewards far beyond those of United States senators and when the doings of glamourous society characters have been glorified in a manner to pale the chronicles of Belshazzar, the ranking name of all is that of the Stork Club.

To millions and millions of people all over the world the Stork symbolizes and epitomizes the de luxe upholstery of quintessentially urban existence. It means fame; it means wealth; it means an elegant way of life among celebrated folk. The Stork is so much of a news institution that it has long since done away with the services of a regular press agent, and news editors and reporters of the New York scene regard it much as they regard the Metropolitan Opera or the Circus. The Stork is the dream of suburbia, a shrine of sophistication in the minds of countless thousands who have never seen it, the fabric and pattern of legend. It supplies copy daily to scores of newspaper paragraphers; cinema spectacles have been built around its premises. It used to be a classic newspaper axiom that a dogfight in Main Street was worth more play than a war in Europe. A fistfight at the Stork is today more newsworthy than an atom bomb. During the second World War the Stork existed in the minds of uncounted scores of thousands of fighting men all over the world as the most desirable place in existence. The record is incontestably available to prove it.

A good deal of highly paid space in coated paper magazines and elsewhere and the intellectual resources of scores of authorities, ranging from Stanley Walker and Katharine Brush to the editors of learned reference books of biography and manners, have been devoted to evaluating the Stork and Mr. Billingsley and what makes them click with such astounding and ever crescent precision. Its breathless success has been variously attributed to the transcendent genius of the proprietor, to his lavishness with material favors and friendship with the reporters, to the Stork's fortunate geographic location, to its cuisine, to its superb disdain for floor shows and even to the favor and occasional patronage of Mrs. Vanderbilt. The record, however, will show that the Stork was fantastically profitable when it was located in Fifty-eighth Street on the wrong side of Fifth Avenue, that numerous other saloon proprietors have set up drinks for the paragraphers without any trace of the Stork's overwhelming prestige, and that Mrs. Vanderbilt also favors with her presence the Metropolitan Opera, a tradition in no way comparable either on a fun basis or financially to the Cub Room.

Nor is Mr. Billingsley altogether infallible. Sometimes his most adroitly fashioned strategies go completely snafu.

Every now and then it is his fond whim to devise a new code of signals by which, without attracting the attention of patrons, he can govern the conduct and the staff of the Stork Club. Recently he dreamed up a new essay in folly through whose agency he hoped to inform his doormen and waiter captains of the status and welcome of arriving guests by a series of code numbers which the master would mutter to an attendant at his elbow and which would be swiftly relayed to the door staff. The number thirteen, for example, signified: "the fellow is poison; give him the bounce;" number one hundred meant: "give him the best of everything and a bottle of champagne on the house," while sixty-five or some such indicated: "stop serving him after the tenth Scotch but give his lady a bottle of free perfume with my compliments." The system worked fine until one evening when an unsuitable patron had been firmly refused admission and shown the door only to reappear a couple of minutes later with a broad leer on his face and on either arm a liberally beribboned and entirely presentable service man whom he had acquired on the sidewalk and whose welcome was universal and obligatory.

Sherman's systems have always had their limitations. A number of years ago he dreamed up a particularly complicated code by which the accustomed messages of hospitality or the bounce were to be relayed by a complicated arrangement of gestures. If the Boss tugged his left ear lobe it meant "out into the night with the goon;" lighting a cigarette signified "a ringside table" or if he blinked his eyes rapidly it informed the captain "let the fellow into the bar but say the Cub Room is full."

The very first night the new order went into effect all hell broke loose at the Stork. The Master absent-mindedly spilled salt, fiddled with the ash tray or waved his napkin to illustrate a conversational point and right away notorious drunks were plied with ardent waters gratis, old friends of the establishment and celebrated names had their hats pushed over their ears and were being urged into the outer darkness and the Cub Room was peopled with folk of no consequence whatsoever. That was the end of *that* system, but instanter!

If the writer of the moment may add his two cents' worth to the symposium on what activates the Stork and makes its functioning

very close to perfection, his guess would be that one of its weighti-
est, albeit intangible, assets is the superb organization of its staff
and the circumstance that Mr. Billingsley has never lost a customer
through failure to estimate a patron's importance, the improper
allocation of tables or any injudicious approach whatsoever. In an
institution serving, often enough, three thousand persons a day,
many of them notables with a complete willingness to be imaginarily
slighted or to turn on the flow of professional temperament, this is
a notable achievement.

And, over and above all considerations, there is the primary
function of the Stork as a night club and restaurant: the service of
liquor and food in that order of importance. These are also the
concern, in what is hoped will be a humane and practical manner,
of this Bar Book. The subject has engaged the attentions of many
learned practitioners of the calling of beautiful letters. Of the
making of many cookbooks and cocktail guides there is no end.
But because drinking in the Stork Club manner is probably repre-
sentative of the most civilized and urbane habits of American tosspots, barring, of course, the mysteries and mannered potations of
such esoteric oenophiles as Les Amis d'Escoffier and the Wine and
Food Society, this essay is devoted to drinking as practiced in the
various parlors, anterooms and state suites of the Stork. It embraces
hardly at all the postured sniffing of debatable vintage years or the
ceremonial evaluations of rare and improbably costly spirits,
although it may be remarked in passing that the Stork's collection
of dated cognacs and other eaux de vie of note is the most extensive
in North America.

Taste in drinking is, quite naturally, everywhere and at all times
conditioned by economic resources, available types of wines and
spirits, climate, society and a score of other more or less ponderable
factors. The various native and Indies rums which were the first

national spirits of the United States in the eighteenth century were almost universally popular because of their immediate availability, their integration to the islands trade in cane and molasses and their suitability to cold climate, outdoor life and generally unheated houses. Champagne became the favorite drink of the nineteenth century Russian nobility because of its costliness and exotic nature, and to lend it an authority lacking through natural fermentation it was heavily fortified for the Russian market with cognacs and other brandies. Madeira was at one time the universal wine among people of manners and position in America because of its trade accessibility to clipper shipping.

Similarly it is quite possible to trace a close parallel between the trend of American life away from the countryside toward cities and the rise in mixed drinks, imported beverages and a general alcoholic sophistication. There are still American frontiers where a drink means only one thing: Bourbon whisky, and the only chaser thinkable is beer or soda water, but these are fast vanishing. The once wicked mixed drink is now almost universal, and in polite circumstance, where the object is to extend the pleasure and usefulness of a drink over the longest possible social and conversational period, the tall mixed drink flourishes luxuriantly. The lore of keeping bar has become enormously complicated for, while the vast preponderance of orders are for drinks which can be numbered on the ten fingers, a knowing barman must be able, instanter and without reference to other authority, to compound any of several hundred stimulating arrangements, and even the conventional stand-bys, Martini cocktails and Scotch highballs, are subject to little variations and the perfections of individual taste and practice.

It is with the end in view of recording the preferences, practices and prejudices of drinkers at the wonderful and legendary mahogany of the Stork Club that this book has been evolved. It is not the record of how Martinis are compounded at the Men's Bar of the Plaza, or how the white aproned experts fling together a Planter's Punch at the Palace in San Francisco or how a whisky toddy is fabricated at the Hurry Back in Salt Lake, the Switch Key in Fort Worth or the Nose Paint Saloon in Durango, Colorado. These splendid shrines have their own local customs and individual ways of doing things, but they are not the ways of the Stork Club.

The Stork Club's drinking has never been accomplished in the cloistered privacy of old gentleman's clubs; it has been orchestrated to sweet music, illuminated by the heat lightning of photographer's flashes and upholstered in broadcloth and starched linen. It has been drinking in the grand manner, guzzling with a panache of chic and elegance, a hoisting of crystal chalices in the secure knowledge that the wit, beauty, chivalry and wealth of the world were doing the identical thing at adjacent tables, each one a location of distinction and reserved for names that make news alone. Make no mistake, drinking at the Stork is neither a shy, anonymous nor retiring occupation. It is a public rite and requires stylish gestures and the distant, barely audible accompaniment of French horns.

Do you hear the French horns calling? I do.          *L.B.*

*Morning*

at the Stork Club...

*It is* a matter of common acceptance that even the most firmly established usages are subject to the mutations of time, and that what was yesterday a practice confined to the far side of the railroad tracks (a part of town often frequented by the best people but always in closed hacks) is today definitely au fait in Mayfair. The concern of men of intelligence is not so much with what may be fashionable as with what is reasonable, and, while the notion of drinking cocktails directly after breakfast may seem at first consideration an eminently unchristian practice, this has not always been the case.

Disregarding as impertinent to the important matter in hand all learned controversy over the origin of the word cocktail, whether it sprung from the Aztec Xochitl or from the custom of compounding the arrangement with a chicken's feather for ornamental panache, the cocktail as it is known today first achieved widespread acceptance, so far as diligent research can establish, in the middle years of the nineteenth century.

It gained favorable mention in the fifties and sixties as the mid-morning slug of the captains of industry and finance on whose waistcoats it was practicable to play games and who rode downtown from Murray Hill to Wall Street after a breakfast which would founder today's fragile souls who face the day fortified by an eye-dropper filled with orange juice and a slice of Melba toast. In the President-Grant-and-Erie-common age drinking was a notably masculine occupation and it went hand in hand with chewing tobacco and owning large stables. Everything was big; the whisky slug was four ounces, the cuspidors in the Astor House might reasonably be confused with umbrella stands, and the business of agitating the liver and stirring the senses into function began early in the day.

Gentlefolk often drank a brandy sling heavily laced with Stoughton's Bitters, a notable cure-all of the times, before descending to breakfast. Hardier if less elegant souls had a slug of rock and rye while shaving and brushed their teeth in a light Moselle. The square hat compartment which was part of every man's chiffonier of the period was often as not devoted, not to father's best gray topper from Yourmans, but to a bottle of Lawrence's Medford Rum, a chummy bedroom companion and an aid in tying the complicated stocks and Ascots then in sartorial favor.

During the ride downtown the pre-breakfast restorative, no matter how liberally applied, tended to die on the captains of finance and industry and a few of the less sensitive of that valiant generation paused at spas previously ascertained and charted near Canal Street before continuing to the shadow of Grace Church, but this was frowned on by the conservative or J. P. Morgan element which maintained that a man should be able to read his own mail, at least the first delivery, unaided by the office staff.

One skirmish with the stock ticker, however, and a whiff of what Jay Gould was doing in the gold market usually set even the Morgan partners to reaching for their hats and telling the receptionist they were just going across the street to the Subtreasury for a few minutes. They invariably returned from the Subtreasury eating a clove.

This practice, mark you, of midmorning refreshment originally carried with it no least suggestion of relinquished moral control or decline in individual deportment. It was as commonly accepted and respectable a ritual at the period of which we write as is the high noon sour or a restorative milk punch today and had about it no implication of devoting the day to fun or chartering a hack to drive to City Island for lunch. Midmorning was the first well-established masculine cocktail hour.

In an age when stem glassware was less common than it is today cocktails were served in what is now known as a Delmonico glass, a practice still observed at Whyte's and a few other old-time restaurants in the financial district, and ran in quantity to the size of a modern sour. Because of its unrivaled tonic qualities as a restorative and element for firming the moral fiber, as well as because of the prevailing American taste for drinks with whisky bases at this time, the classic and standard Manhattan cocktail, precisely as it is served at this red hot minute at the Stork Club, was an almost universal rite until the end of the nineteenth century.

*Manhattan Cocktail:*  ⅔ oz. rye whisky
⅓ oz. Italian vermouth
*Decorate with maraschino cherry, stir, and serve in 3 oz. cocktail glass.*

Whatever may be the present vogue for Martinis, a drink which became firmly established as Londons type gin became more widely available in the United States, make no mistake about it: the Manhattan was the archetypal short mixed drink and blazed a trail for all others to follow. Nor, accomplished bartenders will point out, is it necessary or even advisable to use the finest and oldest proof spirits in making the most acceptable Manhattan. The smoother and sweeter the whisky, the less volume or incisiveness will be possessed by the finished cocktail and it has often been remarked that the most exciting Manhattan is one compounded with ordinary quality bar whisky rather than the rarest overproof article. It is perhaps the only mixed drink where this generality obtains.

There are, of course, a good many redactions and variations of the Martini which depends for its sweetness or dryness on the proportions with which gin and vermouth are used, but the standard and universal dry Martini is still the simplest and most effective mixed drink ever devised:

**Dry Martini:**     ⅔ oz. Londons or dry gin
⅓ oz. French vermouth
*Stir, decorate with olive and serve in 3 oz. cocktail glass.*

The perfect Martini, somewhat smoother and less potent to the taste, is achieved by using the same proportions of gin and vermouth, but equal parts of French and Italian vermouth are used, in other words 1/6 oz. each in the above formula. The Gibson, long a favorite with discriminating, older drinkers, was first, according to the legend, evolved by the late Charles Dana Gibson at the bar of the Plaza Hotel in New York and was made with a pickled onion for ornament instead of the traditional green olive.

A vast deal of pother has from time to time been raised over the almost fanciful advantages of stirring over shaking Martinis. The almost universal custom is for stirring them, but Marco, head barman at New York's celebrated Colony Restaurant, makes a practice of shaking them vigorously and candor compels the admission that the only discernible difference between the two products is that a spooned Martini is crystal clear while a shaken one inclines to a clouded appearance. Bar practice at the Stork favors the noncontroversial stirring or spooning, but the management will oblige by having them compounded in a cement mixer or butter churn if that is what the customer wants. When drinking Martinis, Cookie, the barkeep, remarks, the customer is almost always right.

Other variations are common and many of them legitimate, such as the alternate devised a number of years ago by Steve Hannagan of using a dry sherry instead of vermouth for a particularly lethal Martini, and a drink thoughtfully named for herself by Rosalind Russell, the secret of which should be guarded like that of the atom bomb, but which she is willing the world shall share if she is held blameless of the results:

*Rosalind Russell:*    ⅔ jigger Danish Alborg aquavit
⅓ jigger vermouth or dubonnet
*Shake or spoon and serve in the same manner as a Martini.*

Miss Russell's own comment on this arrangement is: "My father-in-law, Carl Brisson, introduced me to this drink and six months later I married his son!"

In a less heroic generation, however, it must be recorded that few demands are received across the bar of the Stork for cocktails until after the sun has crossed the proverbial yardarm at noon. Public taste in restoratives, pick-me-ups and simple, old-fashioned drinking for pleasure runs more to longer and taller drinks and less to the concentrated essence of life to be encountered in cocktails.

As is entirely natural in such a highly individualized occupation, requirements for morning drinks vary with almost every forenoon drinker. There may be a certain or prevailing similarity of tastes at more conventional hours and the steward can count upon a fairly regular dispensation of, say, Martinis at lunchtime or Daiquiris before dinner, but the A.M. elbow bender is a Maverick, a lone wolf and there is no predicting his vagrant whim or fancy.

If his innards require gentling and the virtues of nourishment at the same time, his requirement may be for a milk punch or fizz with eggs. He may demand the moderate advancement of the governing throttle implicit in a sour or simple highball, or he may call in impassioned tones for the alcoholic equivalent of adrenalin and oxygen, the quick emergency functions of Stinger, Scotch Mist or a Sundowner Cocktail.

It is in the early watches that the knowing and perceptive barkeep must most closely fill the function of physician and adviser. His clients are in humbled or quiescent mood, usually in search of soft words and consolation. By noontime he may be in requisition as adviser on the race track situation and by nightfall, variously in demand as councillor at love, bail bondsman or bouncer, but in the morning his technique is guided by a strictly bedside manner.

Some of the more conventional restoratives during the placid hours when the laundry is delivering the waiter's aprons and the day's beer is cooling in the coils are:

**Milk Punch (plain):**  ½ pt. milk
1 tsp. sugar
*Shake, strain and serve in 12 oz. glass and put little nutmeg on top.*

**Sherry Flip:**  2 oz. sherry wine
1 tsp. sugar
whole egg
*Shake well. Nutmeg on top. Use wine glass.*

**Port Flip:**  2 oz. port wine
1 tsp. sugar
whole egg
*Shake well. Nutmeg on top. Use wine glass.*

**Sherry Eggnog:**

1 egg
2 oz. sherry
1 tsp. sugar
milk
*Shake, strain and serve in tall glass. Nutmeg on top.*

**Baltimore Eggnog:**

1 fresh egg
½ tbsp. fine granulated sugar
¼ jigger brandy
¼ jigger Jamaica rum
½ pt. fresh milk
*Shake well and strain into highball glass. Serve with a grating of nutmeg.*

**Port Eggnog:**

1 egg
2 oz. port wine
1 tsp. sugar
milk
*Shake, strain and serve in tall glass. Nutmeg on top.*

If, by reason of ill-advised research among the flagons the night before, scholarship has triumphed over discretion; if in a word the entire human person resembles nothing so much as what the author of this volume's first city editor, Norton Pratt of the Boston *Telegram* used to define as "a basket of busted bungholes," Burgess Meredith has a cure for it. It's called "London Fog".

**London Fog:**

1½ oz. gin
¼ oz. Pernod's absinthe
*Frappe briskly with shaved ice and serve while still foaming.*

This, of course, is among the more heroic remedies, and a few of the less lethal and drastic cures available to the almost illimitable resources of Cookie are the following:

**Whisky Sour:**

2 oz. whisky
Juice of half lemon
1 tsp. sugar
*Shake, strain and serve in Delmonico glass.*
*Dress with fruit. Squirt of seltzer.*

**Brandy Eggnog:**

1 egg
2 oz. brandy
1 tsp. sugar
milk
*Shake, strain and serve in tall glass with*
*nutmeg on top.*

**Egg Sour:**

1 tsp. fine granulated sugar
3 dashes lemon juice
1 oz. curaçao
1 oz. brandy
1 egg
*Shake with cracked ice and strain into Del-*
*monico glass.*

**Rum Eggnog:**

1 egg
2 oz. rum
1 tsp. sugar
milk
*Shake, strain and serve in tall glass with*
*nutmeg on top.*

**Port Wine Cobbler:**     Fill goblet with fine ice
3 oz. port wine
1 tsp. sugar
*Stir. Decorate with fruit—sprig of mint.*
*Straws.*

Jean Hersholt's version of a perfect pick-me-up is:

**Pick-Me-Up:**     1 oz. French vermouth
1 oz. cherry brandy
¼ oz. dry gin
*Should be served frozen cold in a large cock-*
*tail or Delmonico glass and consumed before*
*it has a chance to warm up.*

This last generality contained in Mr. Hersholt's directions for re-
storing animation to the flagging torso is one which, generally
speaking, applies to all short drinks in the cocktail and sour class
and to the complicated chemistry of pick-me-ups in particular. Old-
time barkeeps had a phrase for it: "Drink it while it's laughing at
you." And that is the way these drinks should be downed, immediately and with dispatch, not lovingly sipped like a liqueur or
allowed to come to a slow boil in the hand like a bankrupt's highball. It is neither the mark of a pig nor an alcoholic to get these
drinks insinuated into the system with a maximum of dexterity
because that is the way they were made to be drunk. The cocktail
never could have come into existence without ice and, to this day,
is notably not in demand in parts of the world where ice is a scarce
commodity. For the record shows that the Falernian of Nero and
other prominent Romans was served chilled with the snows of the
Appenines, but backward communities ever since have resisted the

devisings of refrigeration as in England, where the iced highball is frowned on as on a par with the short jacket in the evening, although civilization is reported slowly to be advancing even within the straitened confines of the Tight Little Island.

Among the more exotic of the restorative category is a sort of bastard Martini evolved by Willard Parker with all the ingredients cockeyed as well as the consumer:

**Parkeroo:**      2 oz. dry sherry
            1 oz. tequila
            twist of lemon peel.
            *Pour this concoction over shaved ice, allow to chill and then pour into pre-chilled champagne coup glass.*

"While painting a picket fence around my house," deposes Mr. Parker, "I discovered that after two Parkeroos I could remain stationary and let the fence revolve around the brush. This will give you an idea!"

No less effective in the realm of non-academic medicine for morning use may be found the following patent nostrums, some of them dating from grandma's day and all of them esteemed as sovereign remedies:

**Rum Toddy:**      1½ oz. Jamaica rum
            1 tsp. sugar
            2 cloves
            slice of lemon
            cinnamon
            *Serve in old-fashioned glass. Add boiling water or cold water as the case may be.*

| | |
|---|---|
| **Sherry Cobbler:** | fill goblet with fine ice |
| | 3 oz. sherry |
| | 1 tsp. sugar |
| | 1 twist lemon peel |
| | add dash of cherry brandy |
| | *Stir. Decorate with fruit, sprig of mint.* |

| | |
|---|---|
| **Morning Glory Fizz:** | 1½ oz. Scotch |
| | 1 tsp. powdered sugar |
| | white of egg |
| | ½ tsp. sugar |
| | *Shake and strain in highball glass. Top with seltzer.* |

| | |
|---|---|
| **Brandy Flip:** | 2 oz. brandy |
| | 1 tsp. sugar |
| | whole egg |
| | *Shake well. Nutmeg on top. Use 4 oz. wine glass.* |

| | |
|---|---|
| **South Side Fizz:** | 1½ oz. gin |
| | juice of half lemon |
| | 2 sprigs of mint |
| | 1 tsp. sugar |
| | *Shake well, strain into highball glass and add seltzer. Decorate with mint.* |

Amidst this scholarly discussion of the uses of advanced medicine in the treatment and cure of you know what, there may well be considered two classic stand-bys which have engaged the speculative attentions of amateurs for many years, the prairie oyster and champagne in various solutions. The prairie oyster is an old-time favorite of such stalwart Irish saloonkeepers as the late, great Dan Moriarity and can be served either with or without the liquor ingredient. It possesses the advantage of extremely hot content along with the nutritional value of raw egg which has long been known as one of the most easily digested foodstuffs:

**Prairie Oyster:**

yolk of egg
1 dash Lea & Perrin's Sauce
red pepper and salt to taste
1½ oz. brandy or madeira
*Serve in old-fashioned glass. Dash of vinegar on top.*

Champagne in the morning is a variously advantageous drink and is practically the only wine which lends itself to absorption twenty-four hours around the clock. About the only standard that can be applied to it is whether or not you are in the mood for the stuff. There are mornings, especially in spring and summer when nature herself is in a clement mood and the shakes are not too overpowering, when nothing seems as auspicious as a very cold bottle of Veuve Clicquot, Mumm's or Charles Heidsick in a very dry cuvée. If the senses are attuned to its reception this can be a happy-making way to start the day, but the slightest discord between the wine and the palate may lead to catastrophe.

There is a school of thought, leaders among whose ranks are such notables as Howard Barnes, the learned drama reporter, Frank Sullivan and the late Berry Wall, which places its faith in that curious admixture of wine and Guinness's stout known as Black Velvet. Their claim that it soothes and gentles the recalcitrant stomach and, all guileful and unperceived, overcomes the jangled nerves is doubtless well founded. On the other hand, there are

those who, confronted with two or three tall glasses of this potation, lapse into what Milt Gross calls "a dip slip". Certainly it is a
heavy arrangement and may result in the achievement of a state of
benign stupefaction by the unwary.

**Black Velvet:**  ½ dry champagne
½ Guinness stout
*Chill these separately and pour them to-*
*gether in equal portions in any available*
*tall glass holding at least a pint.*

Less esoteric than either of the foregoing and, perhaps, more suited
to the purse and pretentions of the average victim of breakfasttime
palsy are some of these, all of which are accessible and some of
them in frequent requisition among the Stork's eleven o'clock
patrons:

**Rob Roy:**  2 oz. Scotch
¾ oz. Italian vermouth
1 dash orange bitters
*Decorate with cherry. Stir and serve in 3 oz.*
*cocktail glass.*

**Scotch Mist:**  1½ oz. Scotch
*With shaved ice — serve in old-fashioned*
*glass. Twist of lemon peel. Serve with straws.*

**Gin Smash:**  1½ oz. gin
crush half lump sugar with 3 sprigs of mint
1 cube ice
fruit
*Serve in old-fashioned glass. Top with selt-*
*zer. Stir.*

Travelers who have made the grand tour to New Orleans, where the absorption of nourishment in liquid form, whether on a medicinal basis or in unabashed search for worldly pleasure and satisfaction, begins at an extremely early hour and where northerners are sometime surprised, although never dismayed, to find the natives drinking Martinis at breakfast, will recall the favorite drinks at such favorite places as the St. Regis, the bar of the St. Charles Hotel, the Old Absinthe House and the long bar of the Roosevelt. Here, before the noonday papers are on the streets, the exquisities of America's oldest urban civilization foregather to contrive ways of losing money on horses and other amiable follies and to command the long, tall drinks that are the essence of urbane and mannered conviviality. The late, lamentable Huey Long, short on virtues as he may have been, at least was the ambassador to the world of the Ramos or Remus fizz and this may be his monument to immortality.

*Ramos Fizz:*        2 dashes of orange flower water
juice of half lemon
2 oz. gin
1 oz. cream
1 egg white
*Shake very well, strain into tall glass and fill with seltzer. Collins glass.*

Governor Long once gave a demonstration of the architecture and consumption of various native Louisiana drinks for the benefit of the reporters and other servants of democracy at the bar of the New Yorker Hotel and, though there were those present who might condemn his brand of politics, there was no one who would even implicitly reproach either his virtuosity as a barkeep or his capacity as his own best customer.

Candor compels the admission that to absorb the native beverages of New Orleans it is most advantageous to be in New Orleans itself. Other atmospheres are vaguely hostile to the leisured formality and circumstance required both for the devising and appreciation of flips and fizzes while much of the charm of their consumption derives from the cool of a sequestered courtyard, such as the Court of the Two Sisters, or from a glimpse, over the shoulders of happy customers, of the dazzling pavement of Canal Street outside. The Stork has them on tap, however, and if such added inducements to their appreciation as gumbo filé, pompano en papillot or fat fresh shrimp right from the Louisiana bayous are required, these too are available on the Stork menu.

Generally speaking, fizzes, flips and cocktails depending for part of their consistencies on the presence of egg, egg white or cream seem closely related to one another and their service appropriate to morning rather than to other times of the day and night when the nature of their economy would tend to impair the appetite for food rather than stimulate it.

| | |
|---|---|
| *Royal Fizz:* | juice of half lemon |
| | 1½ oz. gin |
| | 1 tsp. sugar |
| | 1 egg |
| | *Shake well and strain into highball glass and add seltzer.* |
| | |
| *Silver Fizz:* | juice of half lemon |
| | 1 tsp. sugar |
| | 1½ oz. gin |
| | white of egg |
| | *Shake well and strain into highball glass. Add seltzer.* |

**"New Orleans" Fizz:**  juice of half lime
juice of half lemon
2 dashes orange flower water
1 tsp. sugar
1 oz. sweet cream
2 oz. gin
white of egg
*Shake well, serve in Collins or 12 oz. glass
and add a very little seltzer.*

**Diamond Fizz:**  juice of one lemon
1 tsp. sugar
*Serve in highball glass with one ice cube.
Fill with champagne.*

**Gin Fizz:**  juice of one lemon
1 tsp. sugar
1½ oz. gin
*Shake, strain and serve in highball glass
with 1 cube ice. Fill with syphon.*

**Sloe Gin Fizz:**  juice of half lemon
1 tsp. sugar
1½ oz. sloe gin
*Shake well, strain into highball glass and
add seltzer.*

**Brandy Fizz:**  juice of one lemon
1 tsp. sugar
1½ oz. brandy
*Shake, strain and serve in highball glass
with one cube of ice. Fill with syphon.*

| **Sea Fizz:** | 1½ oz. absinthe |
| | juice of half lemon |
| | 1 tsp. sugar |
| | white of egg |
| | *Shake well, strain into highball glass and add seltzer.* |

| **Coffee Cocktail:** | ¾ oz. brandy |
| | ¾ oz. port wine |
| | 1 tsp. sugar |
| | yolk of egg |
| | *Shake well and serve in wine glass with nutmeg on top.* |

An improvement, as some may think, on the conventional Alexander cocktail is the brainstorm child of Nelson Eddy and he calls it "Alexander the Great".

### Alexander The Great:

½ oz. crème de cacao
½ oz. coffee liqueur
½ oz. fresh cream
1½ oz. vodka
*Shake until cold as Siberia. Watch your Steppes, because more than three of these gives the consumer a wolfish appetite.*

The more conventional Alexander is as follows:

| **Alexander:** | 1½ oz. gin |
| | ¾ oz. crème de cacao |
| | ½ oz. fresh cream |
| | *Shake and serve in 4 oz. wine glass.* |

**White Rose:**

1¾ oz. gin
4 dashes maraschino
4 dashes orange juice
4 dashes lemon juice
egg white
*Shake and serve in 4 oz. wine glass.*

**Eagle Cocktail:**

1½ oz. gin
¾ oz. crème Yvette
juice of half lemon
1 tsp. sugar
white of egg
*Shake and serve in 4 oz. wine glass.*

**Widow's Dream:**

1½ oz. benedictine
whole egg
*Shake well, serve in Delmonico glass and fill with cream.*

**Clover Club:**

1½ oz. gin
4 dashes grenadine
juice of half lemon
white of egg
*Shake and serve in 4 oz. wine glass.*

**Cafe de Paris Cocktail:** 1½ oz. gin
¾ oz. anisette
¾ oz. fresh cream
white of egg
*Shake and serve in 4 oz. wine glass with nutmeg on top.*

**Alexander #2:**  1½ oz. brandy
¾ oz. crème de cacao
½ oz. fresh cream
*Shake and serve in 4 oz. wine glass.*

**Rum Flip:**  2 oz. rum
1 tsp. sugar
whole egg
*Shake well. Nutmeg on top. Use wine glass.*

**Plain Eggnog:**  1 egg
1 tsp. sugar
milk
*Shake, strain and serve in tall glass with nutmeg on top.*

**Blackberry Punch:**  juice of one lemon
1 tsp. fine granulated sugar
2 oz. blackberry liqueur
1 oz. rum
*Shake well with cracked ice and strain into goblet filled with shaved ice. Dress with fruit and serve with straws.*

**Strawberry Fizz:**  juice of half lemon
4 mashed strawberries
½ tsp. sweet cream
1 jigger dry gin
*Shake well with cracked ice and strain into highball glass. Add one ice cube and fill with soda water.*

The repertory of morning drink possibilities is practically endless and, indeed, bounded only by the human imagining and the human capacity for absorption. Old-timers will remember barkeeps of the last generation who made a practice of uncapping a bottle of beer by their bedside before retiring and drinking it, flat and warm, the next morning, in the belief that, since the beer was by now separated from its gaseous content, it would be in prime condition for reabsorbing any gas that it might encounter and notably the gas of the human stomach.

Before taking leave of the subject and moving into the less necessitous and urgent category of noontime life at the Stork it may be wise to consider the function of absinthe as a restorative, pick-me-up and general cure-all. It has been held in high esteem for this purpose by countless informed and knowing drinkers and, in all probability, has its uses. The great drawback to its use in the experience of the author, at least, has been its tendency to dull the appetite for food and consequently delay and diminish the consumption of solid food which, in the end, is the greatest of all restoratives after a night among the pots.

Absinthe by reason of its chemistry is probably the briskest and most violent of bitters and there are many who are charmed with its poetic qualities, its historic antecedents, literary associations and other intangible aspects, and there are also many who admire its wormwood flavor and opalescent optical charms when used merely as a flavoring for drinks with other bases.

If the amateur of its properties can really take it or leave it and shift either to a less treacherous drink or to food itself after a couple, there is probably no pick-me-up in the world comparable for immediate efficacy to an absinthe frappe.

**Absinthe Frappe:**    1½ oz. absinthe, green or white
1 white of egg
1 tsp. sugar
*Frappe briskly with shaved ice and serve frozen cold in a Delmonico glass.*

Sometimes the name of a drink has nothing to do with its content, occasion or potentialities and represents nothing more than the dead hand of tradition or the momentary whim of its originator or popularizer. On other occasions, however, it is indicative of the nature of the consequence of the potation, and such would seem to be the case with several of the absinthe arrangements hereinafter catalogued. Their precise nature may best perhaps be summarized by the opening lines of the "Cocktail Song" which amateurs of scholarly matter will find in its entirety in *The Stag's Hornbook* and other hand volumes of reference:

"The cocktail is a pleasant drink;
It's nice and harmless, I don't think!"

**Commando Cocktail:**    1½ oz. bourbon
¾ oz. triple sec
2 dashes pernod
juice of half lime
*Shake and serve in 3 oz. cocktail glass.*

**Hurricane Cocktail:**    1¼ oz. brandy
¾ oz. pernod
¾ oz. vodka
*Shake and serve in 3 oz. cocktail glass.*

**Absinthe Drip:**          1½ oz. absinthe
                            *Dissolve one lump of sugar, using the French drip spoon, and fill glass with cold water.*

**Absinthe Cocktail:**      1½ oz. absinthe
                            1 white of egg
                            1 tsp. sugar
                            *Shake. Twist of lemon peel on top. Serve in 4 oz. wine glass.*

**Earthquake Cocktail:**    1 oz. gin
                            1 oz. bourbon
                            ¾ oz. absinthe
                            *Shake and serve in 3 oz. cocktail glass.*

To append as a coda to this symphony of thunder a less tumultuous assortment of morning favorites of long standing with moderate tosspots, such traditional long and short ones as sloe gin rickies, Tom Collinses, Daiquiris and claret lemonade are all of them at once convivial, restorative and stimulating to the wit and intellect without being conducive to tumult or public commotion.

**Sloe Gin Rickey:**        1½ oz. sloe gin
                            *Insert juice of half lime and rind in highball glass. Fill glass with seltzer and stir.*

**Tom Collins:**            2 cubes ice
                            juice of one small lemon
                            1 tsp. sugar
                            2 oz. gin
                            *Use tall glass. Fill with soda and shake.*

**Daiquiri:**

2 oz. silver rum
juice of half lime
1 tsp. sugar
*Shake well and serve in 3 oz. cocktail glass.*

**Claret Lemonade:**

juice of one lemon
1 tsp. sugar
cracked ice in tall glass
top with 3 oz. claret wine
fruit
dash of seltzer
*Serve with a straw in Collins glass and decorate with fruit.*

And on this note of gentility and restraint it may be announced by the management that luncheon is served.

at the Stork Club...

# Transition

*Transition*, in any occupation as delicately balanced as that of purveying or consuming things to drink, can never be abrupt and must be achieved by almost imperceptible degrees. For this reason the passage of time from morning through noon and the change in clientele from those impelled by urgency or social inclination to a few quick ones in the morning to the Stork's patrons who begin drifting in on the imponderable margins of lunchtime is never dramatic. The tides that ebb and flow past the plush rope and through the front bar are hardly ever well defined or abruptly demarked with the single exception of theater hour which is, all over New York, a more or less mathematically fixed time of transition when an old order, nightly and on matinee days, gives place to new.

For this reason the subdivision of this Book of the Hours of the Stork into the three dominant periods of the drinking and eating day and night is almost entirely arbitrary, a device to establish a pattern of chronology and editorial order rather than a factual representation of circumstance. To the casual and uninstructed eye there would probably be small visible difference between the patronage of the bar at one in the afternoon and eight in the evening except for the presence of evening attire among the customers. The knowing observer would note, however, an absence of professional and celebrity faces in the middle of the day, when a feminine clientele is notably in possession, and a corresponding rise in the index of masculinity after dark. It would take a real expert or at least an amateur of New York drinking habits to tell the hour of day from the nature of the drinks being passed across the bar by Cookie and his assistants. There are enough Martinis at midnight and a sufficient flow of champagne at midday to addle the wits of the uninitiate.

As has been suggested above, the midday clientele of the Stork is considerably different from that say of such downtown resorts of masculinity as the Recess Club or Whyte's in that the patrons are predominantly feminine and, even in an age when women's tastes in drinks has begun to approximate if not exactly duplicate that of men, the run of orders is more on the elaborate side than is likely to be the case later in the day.

Glamourous and worldly Gloria Swanson, a celebrity unabashed in her tastes and determined on the best, likes to start the day with what, within the memory of the author used to be known on the Continent as "King's Ruin," because it was the traditional favorite of so many of the old, bearded kings of Europe who used to frequent Foyot's, the Café de Paris, Maxim's and the Ritz in the days when the going for kings was good. Miss Swanson prefers to call it more elegantly a champagne cocktail even though she commands it served in a tall Tom Collins glass:

### Champagne Cocktail Gloria Swanson:

> 1 pint iced champagne, very dry
> 2 oz. the best cognac
> twist of lemon peel
> *Served in a tall Tom Collins glass with a cube or two of ice.*

Other schools of thought like the same drink in modified containers and with a dash of Angostura Bitters and the author has seen it prepared for such exquisite drinkers as the late King of Spain with a teaspoon of strawberry liqueur in place of the sugar and bitters.

*Champagne Cocktail:*    1 lump sugar, saturated with Angostura
                                        bitters
                                    1 cube of ice
                                    twist of lemon peel
                                    *Fill with chilled champagne and serve in champagne glass.*

In the same family as the various versions of champagne cocktail is the celebrated French 75, an elixir which, if it did not actually have its origin in the first of the German wars, at least came to the general attention of American drinkers at that time and was immediately enshrined in the pharmacopoeia of alcohol artistry in the United States upon the conclusion of hostilities in 1919.

*"French 75":*    2 oz. gin
                            1 tsp. powdered sugar
                            juice of half lemon
                            cracked ice
                            *Top with champagne and serve in tall glass.*

Some less exotic but nonetheless popular noontime cocktails follow:

*Cooperstown:*    1¾ oz. gin
                            ½ oz. French vermouth
                            ½ oz. Italian vermouth
                            2 sprigs mint
                            *Shake, strain well and serve in 3 oz. cocktail glass.*

**Dubonnet Cocktail:**    1⅓ oz. dubonnet
1⅓ oz. gin
*Twist of lemon peel. Stir and serve chilled in 3 oz. cocktail glass.*

**Clover Leaf:**    1½ oz. gin
4 dashes grenadine
juice of half lemon
white of egg
mint leaves
*Shake and serve in 4 oz. wine glass with sprig of mint on top.*

**Bermuda Cocktail:**    1¾ oz. gin
¾ oz. peach brandy
2 dashes grenadine
2 dashes orange juice
*Shake and serve in 3 oz. cocktail glass.*

**Bacardi Cocktail:**    2 oz. Bacardi rum
juice of half lime
1 dash grenadine
*Shake and serve in 3 oz. cocktail glass.*

**Cuban Cocktail:**    1½ oz. brandy
¾ oz. apricot brandy
juice of half lime
*Shake well and serve in 3 oz. cocktail glass.*

**Panama Cocktail:**    1¼ oz. brandy
¾ oz. cream
¾ oz. crème de cacao
*Shake and serve in 4 oz. cocktail glass.*

***Cotillion Cocktail:***    1½ oz. bourbon
    ½ oz. triple sec
    ½ oz. orange juice
    ½ oz. lemon juice
    1 dash rum
    *Shake and serve in 3 oz. cocktail glass.*

Long ago in the early Scott Fitzgerald era when collegiate youth down for the weekend from New Haven had never heard of a yet-to-be-born Stork Club, they did their hoisting at a variety of places dominated, over the years of the early twenties, by Matt Winkle's at 381 Park Avenue and the celebrated resort of Dan and Mort Moriarity at 216 East Fifty-eighth Street. The lore and legends of the age are available in other and better suited repositories than here, but one of the institutions of a time when Connie Bennett was the pin-up girl of the Plaza Grill on Saturday afternoons and the tea dance was in its finest flower was the practice of pooling the resources of ten or a dozen undergraduates to reserve a single bedroom at the Commodore Hotel. This served to shave, change to dinner attire and park their luggage in for the weekend, and, by a few simple expedients, such as dismantling the bed of its double mattresses and wedging two customers in the bathtub, as many as fifteen were able to spend the night in such an apartment with a maximum of discomfort and minimum of cash outlay.

Sunday noontime was invariably one of remorse, stock taking, bail raising and attempts to quicken the unidentified dead found in a coma beside the laundry hamper and the sole clue to whose identity was a return ticket to New Haven in the pocket of a Brooks dinner jacket. Usually three or four quarts of gin could be raised among the bottle scarred veterans of Saturday night at the Palais Royal, and it was rendered potable by the simple expedient of calling upon room service for an appropriate quantity of orange water ice and mixing the two in whatever vessels lent themselves handily to the purpose. A solid metal wastebasket was generally approved as ideal, and the stimulant resulting was known to a whole generation of scholars as

### Commodore Bedroom:

1 qt. Gordon's gin
1 qt. orange water ice
*Shake together in a pitcher or other chalice without other ingredient, as the water ice provides both chilling and mixer for the gin.*

It will be at once perceived that this was a crude and rough-and-ready makeshift for two cocktails which once exercised a considerable hold upon the general imagination, although of recent years they have been supplanted by other favorites.

### Bronx Cocktail:

1 oz. gin
¾ oz. sweet vermouth
¾ oz. French vermouth
¼ oz. orange juice
*Shake and serve in 3 oz. cocktail glass.*

### Orange Blossom:

2 oz. gin
¾ oz. orange juice
*Shake and serve in 3 oz. cocktail glass.*

Another miscellaneous clutch of cocktails which Mr. Billingsley's day-shift Ganymedes report as being in current high favor with the carriage trade include:

| *White Lady:* | 1½ oz. gin |
| | ¾ oz. cointreau |
| | juice of half lemon |
| | egg white |
| | *Shake and serve in 4 oz. wine glass.* |

| *Gin Daisy:* | juice of half lemon |
| | 4 dashes of grenadine |
| | 1½ oz. gin |
| | *Serve in goblet with fine ice, fruit, squirt of* |
| | *seltzer. Straws.* |

**El Presidente Cocktail:**

1½ oz. rum
1¼ oz. French vermouth
2 dashes grenadine
twist of orange peel
*Shake and serve in 3 oz. cocktail glass.*

Should the matter of food, at an appropriate pause in the rounds of restoratives, rear its dainty head at this juncture, the management of the Stork stands ready and willing to purvey certain dishes which have become favorites with luncheon patrons and half a dozen of which are here briefly mentioned. All standard variations on the luncheon theme may be taken for granted as available on the ample house menu: these are specialties and indigenous to the premises at No. 3 East Fifty-third Street.

Omelette Steve Hannagan was named for one of the Stork's first patrons, oldest inhabitants and the closest confident of the management for no more elusive reason than that Mr. Hannagan favors his omelette garnished with diced mushrooms, fried eggplant and stewed tomatoes.

Shirred Eggs Bibesco are compounded with a julienne of tongue, mushrooms and the best Perigordine truffles in a Madeira sauce, while Scrambled Eggs Divette are lovingly chafed in fresh butter and thick cream and garnished with sliced Louisiana shrimps of outsize proportions in a shrimp sauce with asparagus tips.

If something more robust is in order, there is Minced Chicken Montlord: whole slices of thick white meat in cream sauce, illustrated with truffles and mushrooms and interlaced with Virginia ham in long slices.

Calves Liver Hommil is a familiar saute of liver with the added feature supplied by sauce Smitaine, while Veal Sweetbreads Rose Marie are broiled with half tomato, French fried eggplant, the heads of fresh mushrooms and Madeira sauce.

The tally of noontime drinks which pass as currency over the square mahogany in the Stork front room are as various as the personalities of the "name" patrons who command them, running from the simple double Scotch and soda which is invariable with Edward Arnold, the brandy and cognac highball described elsewhere but known to George Sanders as "Saint's Halo," and the double glass of California claret affected by Nigel Bruce to the secret concoction made for her friends by Dame May Whitty and called "Dame's Downfall," which not even Cookie by counting the bottles called for has been able to analyze, and Brock Pemberton's simple and Spartan preference, "grape or apple."

Other "over the yardarm" calls, the record attests, frequently come for:

*Jack Rose:*  2 oz. applejack
juice of half lemon
4 dashes grenadine
*Shake and serve in 3 oz. cocktail glass.*

**Gin Sling:**

1½ oz. gin
sugar to taste
*Serve in 8 oz. highball glass with 2 cubes of ice. Fill with carbonic. Twist of lemon peel.*

**Whisky Daisy:**

juice of half lemon
4 dashes of grenadine
1½ oz. whisky
*Serve in goblet with fine ice, fruit, squirt of seltzer.*

**John Collins:**

use tall glass
2 cubes ice
juice of one small lemon
1 tsp. of sugar
2 oz. Holland gin
*Fill with soda and stir.*

**Applejack Sour:**

2 oz. applejack
juice of half lemon
1 tsp. sugar
*Shake, strain and serve in Delmonico glass. Dress with fruit. Squirt of seltzer.*

**September Morn Cocktail:**

2 oz. Bacardi rum
juice of half lime
4 dashes grenadine
*Add egg white. Shake and serve in 4 oz. wine glass.*

| | |
|---|---|
| ***Star Daisy:*** | juice of half lemon<br>4 dashes grenadine<br>1½ oz. applejack<br>*Serve in goblet with fine ice, fruit, squirt of seltzer.* |
| ***Rum Daisy:*** | juice of half lemon<br>4 dashes of grenadine<br>1½ oz. rum<br>*Serve in goblet of fine ice. Fruit and squirt of seltzer.* |
| ***Doctor Cocktail:*** | 1½ oz. Swedish punch<br>juice of half lime<br>¾ oz. Jamaica rum<br>*Shake and serve in 3 oz. cocktail glass.* |
| ***Amer-Picon Highball:*** | 2 oz. Amer-Picon<br>¾ oz. grenadine or lemon syrup<br>1 cube ice<br>*Serve in highball glass. Fill with syphon. Stir.* |
| ***Depth Bomb:*** | 1½ oz. apple brandy<br>1 oz. brandy<br>4 dashes grenadine<br>4 dashes lemon juice<br>*Shake and serve in 4 oz. wine glass.* |

Generally speaking, the history of the origins and evolution of a particular drink are lost in the shades of antiquity or of last evening as the case may be. Not so the Ward Eight. Perhaps because it came into being in a community noted for the orderliness of its thoughts and its fastidious devotion to history, perhaps because of the circumstance that it first saw the light of day in premises particularly favored by newspaper men and other literati, we know where and approximately when the Ward Eight first leaped at the throat of an astonished world.

Locke-Ober's Winter Place Wine Rooms, a venerable Boston institution and still to this day the town's foremost restaurant, tap-room and resort of masculinity, was located in the eighties as it is today in Winter Place, a short news running between Temple Place and Winter Street or, if you prefer, between the Five Cent Savings Bank and Stowell the jeweler. But a stone's throw from the Massachusetts State House on Beacon Hill and famed for its lobster Savannah and planked steaks, it was natural that Locke's should be a resort of politicians and followers of the political scene. Locke's was not and is not in Boston's Ward Eight, but in the period under consideration Ward Eight was a dominant political subdivision of the community and it was natural that a new drink should be christened for this powerful arrondissement. Although the fame of the Ward Eight was carried afar, it remained and is to this day a particular favorite in Boston and, if the thirsty enquirer is in the vicinity of Brimstone Corner, he can conveniently drop by Locke's, admire the oldest cash register in North America, the Tom and Jerry machine, the splendid barroom nude, and have a Ward Eight in the scene of its origin and first fame.

*Ward Eight:*        2 oz. rye
juice of half lemon
4 dashes grenadine
*Shake and serve in tall glass with cracked ice, fruit.*

As a geographic alternative to this Old Colony highball there is always available:

**New Yorker Cocktail:**  2 oz. rye
juice of half lime
1 tsp. sugar
1 dash grenadine
twist of orange peel
*Shake and serve in 3 oz. cocktail glass.*

For no visible regional reason or logic, it was a New Orleans drink which for many years and when built around a substantial base of one of the bourbons listed by S. S. Pierce, the Boston grocers, was a ranking favorite on the New Haven's crack five o'clock, the Merchant's Limited, on the New York-Boston run.

**Sazarac:**  1 dash pernod in old-fashioned glass
1 lump sugar saturated with Peychaud
    bitters
1 cube ice
twist of lemon peel
twist of orange peel
1½ oz. bourbon
*Stir.*

**Mamie Taylor:**  2 cubes ice in tall glass
2 oz. Scotch
slice lemon
1 split ginger ale
*Stir.*

**Gin and Tonic:**　　2 oz. gin
　　　　　　　　　　2 cubes of ice
　　　　　　　　　　slice of lemon
　　　　　　　　　　*Serve in tall glass. Fill with tonic water and stir.*

**National Cocktail:**　2 oz. rum
　　　　　　　　　　3 dashes apricot brandy
　　　　　　　　　　½ oz. pineapple juice
　　　　　　　　　　3 dashes lime juice
　　　　　　　　　　*Shake and serve in 3 oz. cocktail glass.*

Students of local habits and customs may, at somewhat greater length than is here practicable, enquire into the reasons for the ever-rising curve in the chart of the pale cocktail rums and sugar brandies which during the past twenty years have emerged so largely on the American imagination. One reason, obviously, has been the tremendous advertising and promotion campaigns launched by the first and still the dominant manufacturer of sugar brandies, the Cuban firm of Bacardi. Another has been their price which, generally speaking, has been under those of other comparable spirits. A third may well be the feminine factor in public drinking, since it is universally acknowledged that the thin consistency combined with the special suitability of Cuban type rums for mixing with fruits and sugar have a strong appeal to women's taste.

A more oblique angle may be the shrewd approach which was made by the manufacturers and distributors of pale rums through the agency of snob appeal and name publicization. With a knowing eye, Cuban rums, after they had been "discovered" by wealthy travelers and tourists, were first launched in New York and other centers of style, sophistication and manners. The first Cuba Libre the author ever encountered was being drunk by George Jean Nathan in the super-elegant purlieus of the Colony Restaurant and it was from such beginnings as this that the Frozen Daiquiri became as familiar a household property in Social Circle, Georgia, and Fort Madison, Iowa, as the Hoover vacuum cleaner.

The Stork will compound as many drinks with Cuban rums as there are days in the year, but the three which are as dominant in their field as Martinis or Scotch and soda in theirs are:

*Frozen Daiquiri:*     2 oz. silver rum
juice of half lime
1 tsp. sugar
dash of maraschino
shaved ice
*Use electric mixer. Serve unstrained in champagne glass with short straws.*

*Cuba Libre:*     2 oz. rum
insert juice of half lime and rind in tall glass
2 cubes ice
Fill with Coca Cola
*Stir.*

*"MacArthur" Cocktail:*
1½ oz. Bacardi rum
3 dashes Jamaica rum
¾ oz. triple sec or cointreau
1 dash egg white
*Shake and serve in 4 oz. wine glass.*

Allied to by the common ancestry of the cane but as various in their generations as the names under which they are sold are the more traditional molasses rums which, generally speaking, are higher in flavor and alcoholic content than Cuban rums, darker in color, more pungent of aroma and more sanctioned by long usage as a world commodity. Even to attempt a catalogue of their types would be a Herculean labor, but a few of the more common varieties are Jamaica, Haitian, Demerara, Barbados, Antigua, Virgin Islands, San Domingan, New England, Canadian, Charleston and St. Pierre.

The enormous versatility of molasses rums and the endless changes that can be rung on their combination with other flavors, spirits and bases, have made their use popular over the centuries with all classes of drinkers so that the generic term rum has become synonymous with the word liquor. Rum, perhaps, most commonly suggests punch, but it is, to many an expert and knowing palate, the most distinguished of all bases for refreshment in cocktail form.

*Olympia Cocktail:*  
1½ oz. rum (Virgin Islands type)  
1 oz. cherry brandy  
juice of half lime  
*Shake and serve in 3 oz. cocktail glass.*

*Honey Bee:*  
2 oz. Jamaica rum  
¼ oz. honey  
½ oz. lemon juice  
*Shake and serve in 3 oz. cocktail glass.*

*Jamaica Rum Cocktail:*  
2 oz. Jamaica rum  
juice of half lime  
1 tsp. sugar  
*Shake and serve in 3 oz. cocktail glass.*

**Santa Cruz Daisy:**

juice of half lime
2 oz. rum (Santa Cruz type)
3 dashes simple syrup
3 dashes Maraschino
*Serve in goblet with finely shaved ice. Garnish with fruit and top with a squirt of soda water.*


**Rum Sling:**

1½ oz. Jamaica rum
2 dashes Angostura bitters
*Serve in highball glass with cracked ice. Fill with carbonic. Twist of lemon peel. Stir.*


**Planter's Punch:**

⅓ oz. lemon juice
¾ oz. orange juice
4 dashes curaçao
2 oz. Jamaica rum
*Shake and strain into tall glass filled with shaved ice. Decorate with fruit and serve with straws.*


**Mojito Highball:**

2 oz. rum
1 tsp. sugar
juice of half lime and rind
1 cube ice
*Serve in highball glass. Fill with soda. Decorate with 3 sprigs of rind. Stir.*


If none of the foregoing compounds can abate the grief of a stormy morning, Cookie may prescribe for the drooping customer a very special pick-me-up dreamed up in a bemused moment by Ralph Bellamy and known as

### "The Bellamy Scotch Sour":

3 oz. orange juice
2 oz. lemon juice
6 oz. Scotch whisky
1 tsp. honey
1 dash Angostura bitters
*Frappe until frozen cold in a Waring mixer and serve with a piece of preserved ginger on a stick. This, says Mr. Bellamy in a triumph of understatement, is a drink for lazy Sunday afternoons and requires no superselling.*

If no such powerful reviver-from-the-dead is required you might try some of these:

### Remsen Cooler:

2 oz. gin
1 cube ice
peel rind of lemon in spiral form
1 split soda
*Serve in tall glass and stir.*

### American Beauty:

3 dashes white crème de menthe
½ oz. orange juice
½ oz. grenadine syrup
½ oz. French vermouth
½ oz. brandy
*Shake, top with port wine and serve in 4 oz. wine glass.*

**Sundowner:**

1½ oz. brandy
¾ oz. Van Der Hum Liqueur
4 dashes lemon juice
4 dashes orange juice
*Shake and serve in 3 oz. cocktail glass.*

**Admiral Cocktail:**

1½ oz. gin
1 oz. cherry cordial
juice of half lime
*Shake and serve in 3 oz. cocktail glass.*

**Between-the-Sheets:**

¾ oz. rum
¾ oz. brandy
¾ oz. cointreau
juice of half lemon
*Shake and serve in 4 oz. wine glass.*

**Lone Tree Cocktail:**

2 oz. gin
¾ oz. Italian vermouth
*Squeeze orange peel on top, stir and serve in 3 oz. cocktail glass.*

**Gimlet Cocktail:**

1⅓ oz. gin
1⅓ oz. orange juice
*Shake with shaved ice and serve in 3 oz. cocktail glass.*

**Bahamas Highball:**

2 oz. gin
1 oz. French vermouth
1 slice lemon
tonic water
*Serve in highball glass. Stir.*

**B.V.D. Cocktail:**    1¾ oz. applejack
1 oz. Italian vermouth
*Use old-fashioned glass. Stir.*

**Apricot Cocktail:**    1½ oz. apricot brandy
1 oz. gin
2 dashes lemon juice
2 dashes orange juice
*Shake and serve in 3 oz. cocktail glass.*

**Santa Anita:**    1½ oz. Scotch
*Shake with cracked ice and serve in old-fashioned glass. Twist of lemon peel.*

**Manuel Quezon Cocktail:**
1½ oz. apple and honey
¾ oz. triple sec
juice of half lime
*Shake and serve in 3 oz. cocktail glass*

If, by the time this point is reached in the Stork's catalogue of vinous and spirituous offerings, either the reader or the bar patron is inclined, in the interest of complete equilibrium, to command solid food, the chef's suggestion for the day may variously embrace:

**Bluefish Saute Sherman or Stork Club:**
Bluefish saute with plain spinach, sliced mushrooms and Meuniére Sauce.

**Veal Chop Saute Concorde:**
Veal chop saute in butter. Garnished with carrots Vichy, mashed potatoes, new peas, Madeira Sauce.

### Baby Lamb Boulangere:

Roast Baby Lamb. Garnished with glaced small onions and salted pork and potatoes Rissole. Mint Sauce.

### Noisette of Lamb Lavalliere:

Noisette of Lamb in butter garnished with julienne of mushrooms and truffles. Puree of celery, Madeira Sauce.

### Veal Cutlet Gismonda:

Breaded Veal Cutlet with half bread crumbs and half grated Parmisan cheese, saute in butter, garnished with plain spinach, sliced mushrooms. Madeira Sauce.

### Lamb Kidney Saute Cabaret:

Lamb Kidney Saute, Red Wine Sauce. Garnished with small onions, mushrooms, and salted pork.

On the other hand the resources of the bar staff, based on the tastes of customers at the mahogany and the imaginations of generations of serious-minded drinkers, are by no means exhausted by the brief foregoing summaries, which are intended more in the nature of a précis than any definitive handbook. At the risk of making this copy read like the "also among those present" paragraph at the end of a newspaper society item, among those still available, and in demand as afternoon sets in are:

### Shamrock Cocktail:

1½ oz. Irish whisky
1 oz. French vermouth
3 dashes green crème de menthe
3 dashes green Chartreuse
*Stir and serve in 3 oz. cocktail glass.*

**Casino Cocktail:**

2 oz. gin
4 dashes maraschino
4 dashes orange juice
4 dashes lemon juice
*Shake and serve in 3 oz. cocktail glass.*

**Allies Cocktail:**

1¾ oz. gin
1 oz. French vermouth
dash Kümmel
*Serve in 3 oz. cocktail glass.*

**Flying Fortress:**

1 oz. brandy
¾ oz. vodka
½ oz. absinthe
½ oz. triple sec
*Shake and serve in 4 oz. wine glass.*

**Bamboo Cocktail:**

2 oz. dry sherry
¾ oz. Italian vermouth
*Stir and serve in 3 oz. cocktail glass.*

**Boomerang:**

1 oz. rye
¾ oz. French vermouth
¾ oz. Swedish Punch
2 dashes lemon juice
1 dash Angostura bitters
*Serve in 4 oz. wine glass.*

**Angel's Kiss:**

⅔ oz. crème de cacao
⅓ oz. sweet cream on top
*Use cordial glass.*

**Blackout:**

1¾ oz. gin
¾ oz. blackberry brandy
juice of half lime
*Shake and serve in 3 oz. cocktail glass.*

**Devil Cocktail:**

1⅓ oz. brandy
1⅓ oz. green crème de menthe
*Shake and serve in 3 oz. cocktail glass.*

**Whist Cocktail:**

1½ oz. rum
½ oz. applejack
¾ oz. Italian vermouth
*Shake and serve in 3 oz. cocktail glass.*

*Night*

at the Stork Club...

*It is* a cliche of monstrous proportions to remark that day begins at dusk for the Stork Club, but such is indeed the case, and the daylight skirmishes with pots and pans which have been instigated by casual customers have been, in actual fact, a mere rehearsal for the tumult and industry which sets in after six in the evening. Although the Stork is, from the actual record, something less of a night club than it is of a restaurant and less of either than it is a rendezvous of celebrities who may incidentally care to drink, eat and dance, its fame has been founded as a night club and as a night club it has flourished mightily in the public imagination.

The circumstance that there has never been a floor show, the identifying hallmark of any night club ever before heard of, simply doesn't abate the Stork's confusing reputation as a cabaret. More than a hundred patrons or shoppers after amusement enquire, on an average evening, when the floor show starts and are graveled to find there is none, but it is impossible to disabuse suburbia of the notion that the dancing girls will soon come on, and Mr. Billingsley's vicars merely go on denying it year in and year out. In a way, Mr. Billingsley himself is responsible for the legend since, from time to time, he has inaugurated miniature balloon ascensions from which thousand dollar bills have been showered upon the customers, and these and other follies of a similar Tiffanyesque nature have done nothing to discourage the widespread notion that all hell is constantly on tap at No. 3 East Fifty-third Street. There is always an optimistic fringe of customers who persist in the delusion that promptly at midnight Ted Husing, in a gold lamé tailcoat, will shoot Bill Corum right in the lobby and that after that a chorus of unearthly Powers models will distribute platinum cigarette cases to the gentlemen present and platina fox stoles to the ladies.

Meanwhile the accustomed and initiate patrons go about their business of gulping and guzzling the best food and drink ever served in any New York night club since Lillian Russell was a tot, and what they gulp and guzzle is the concern of this particular and scholarly thesis.

As has been suggested elsewhere, human determination and free will being what they are, there is no regulating what drinks will suit the taste of whom at what hour, and the best that can be done is to marshal the resources of Cookie's bar in something that may be a reasonable simulacrum of sound taste and probable demand. Scores of patrons of the Stork, after all, command nothing stronger than Poland water or lemon squash, but they are not the proper concern of the moment.

The approach of the dinner hour, which in New York varies between seven o'clock and midnight, is the signal for unloosing Niagaras of Scotch and soda and cloudbursts of Martinis and old-fashioneds. And if you object to the fruit salad, festoons of maraschino cherries, flotsam and jetsam of orange rind and canopies of Japanese parasols and American flags which are served with old-fashioned cocktails in many places, it is possible to obviate all this nuisance value by simply asking for a bourbon toddy. At Jack Bleeck's Artists and Writers saloon hard by the *Herald Tribune* and in such Hollywood outposts as Mike Romanoffs and Dave Chasen's, it is known for no discoverable reason as a "gag", but its common term is bourbon toddy and by such it goes elsewhere in the land.

**Bourbon Toddy:**    1 lump of sugar saturated with Angostura
        bitters
twist of lemon
2 oz. bourbon whisky
1 oz. water
2 cubes ice
*The sugar should be ground to syrup in the
water with a muddler and the whisky and
ice added after that.*

In its origin and, to the minds of gastronomic purists, the cocktail was originally intended as a brief drink, a quick aperitif to stimulate appetite and stiffen the flagging gustatory senses, but it has passed into accustomed usage as a drink to be absorbed in considerable quantity despite the admonitions of the judicious. A few from the Stork Club's almost illimitable bar book follow at random:

**Parisian Cocktail:**    1½ oz. gin
1 oz. French vermouth
3 dashes crème de cassis
*Shake and serve in 3 oz. cocktail glass.*

**Mary Pickford Cocktail:**
2 oz. rum
¾ oz. pineapple juice
3 dashes grenadine
*Shake and serve in 3 oz. cocktail glass.*

**Rose Cocktail:**    2 oz. French vermouth
½ oz. Kirsch
¼ oz. grenadine
*Stir well and serve in 3 oz. cocktail glass.*

**Millionaire Cocktail:**  1¾ oz. sloe gin
½ oz. apricot brandy
½ oz. Jamaica rum
1 dash grenadine
*Shake and serve in 4 oz. wine glass.*

**Bombay Cocktail:**  1¼ oz. brandy
¾ oz. Italian vermouth
¾ oz. French vermouth
2 dashes curaçao
*Shake and serve in 3 oz. cocktail glass.*

**Ruby Cocktail:**  2 oz. gin
3 dashes grenadine
¾ oz. applejack
*Shake and serve in 3 oz. cocktail glass.*

**Presidente Cocktail:**  1⅓ oz. rum
1⅓ oz. Italian vermouth
twist of orange peel
*Shake and serve in 3 oz. cocktail glass.*

**Miami Cocktail:**  2 oz. rum
¾ oz. cointreau
4 dashes lemon juice
*Shake and serve in 3 oz. cocktail glass.*

It has been remarked elsewhere and may profitably be repeated that the food at the Stork is such as frequently engages the interest of diners who are in no way concerned for the celebrities present and wouldn't know Ann Sheridan if they saw her. Long ago as a practical protest against the school of anesthetized gastronomy which insisted that nothing but scrambled eggs and bacon should be included on a night club menu, Mr. Billingsley went all out for the pleasure and satisfaction of those of his guests whose idea of dinner or supper was something beside salami on rye. At one time the Billingsley support of transcendental gastronomy included the maintenance of a daily airplane service between Florida and New York for the ferrying to the Stork of live stone crabs, fresh Gulf pompano and other rare and costly viands from tropic waters. It was Mr. Billingsley who, to the rage and consternation of competitors in the restaurant business, inaugurated the presence at each table of monstrous mounds of gigantic ripe olives and sheaves of fresh Boston Market celery.

The menu has bristled from year to year with game birds from the grouse moors of Scotland, pheasant en plumage, firkins of pâté de foie and casks of Caspian caviar. The waiters tottered under chateaubriands of outsize proportions culled from prize-winning beeves, and the eyes of patrons lovingly caressed menus awash with soups, sorbets and souffles reminiscent of Foyot's in the great days and of Claridge's in London during the spring seasons before the wars.

Three fish dishes which are the pride of the Stork's chef are Mousse of Sole Washington, Broiled Pompano Tyrolienne and Baked Lobster Excelsior. Mousse of Sole, which was first successfully evolved by the great Escoffier at the Savoy in London and has been universally hailed by gourmets as one of the triumphs of modern culinary art because of the difficulty of retaining in concentrated form the flavor of so delicate a fish, is at the Stork poached and garnished with Lobster a l'Americaine and ornamented with diced mushrooms and truffles.

The pompano is broiled and ornamented with a sauce of French onions and stewed tomatoes, while the lobster is a conventional half shell baked with mushroom sauce in the bottom of the shell, a filling of chopped lobster, fresh butter and celery knob and covered and glacéd with American sauce.

A further assortment of bar compounds which the Stork stands ready at a moment's notice to compound before the happy customer begins wading around in the fish course includes:

*Czarina:*  
1 oz. vodka  
¾ oz. apricot brandy  
½ oz. French vermouth  
½ oz. Italian vermouth  
*Shake and serve in 3 oz. cocktail glass.*

*Aviation Cocktail:*  
2 oz. gin  
juice of half lemon  
4 dashes maraschino  
*Shake and serve in 3 oz. cocktail glass.*

*Diplomat Cocktail:*  
1¾ oz. French vermouth  
1 oz. Italian vermouth  
dash maraschino  
*Stir and serve in 3 oz. cocktail glass.*

*Tovarich:*  
1½ oz. vodka  
1 oz. Kümmel  
juice of half lime  
*Shake and serve in 3 oz. cocktail glass.*

*Duplex:*  
1⅓ oz. French vermouth  
1⅓ oz. Italian vermouth  
dash Angostura bitters  
*Stir and serve in 3 oz. cocktail glass.*

**American Flag Cordial:**

⅓ oz. grenadine
⅓ oz. maraschino
⅓ oz. crème Yvette
*Pour very carefully. Use cordial glass.*

**Royal Smile:**

1¾ oz. gin
¾ oz. applejack
4 dashes grenadine
juice of half lime
*Shake and serve in 3 oz. cocktail glass.*

**Southern Comfort Cocktail:**

1¾ oz. Southern Comfort
juice of half lime
¾ oz. orange liqueur
*Shake and serve in 3 oz. cocktail glass.*

**Paradise Cocktail:**

1¼ oz. gin
¾ oz. apricot brandy
¾ oz. orange juice
*Shake and serve in 3 oz. cocktail glass.*

**Greenbrier Cocktail:**

1⅓ oz. gin
1⅓ oz. Italian vermouth
2 sprigs mint
*Shake well, strain and serve in 3 oz. cocktail glass.*

The Sidecar was, to the best of the knowledge and belief of the author, invented by Frank, steward and senior barkeep of the celebrated Paris Ritz Bar during the golden age of the early twenties.

In an era when Joe Zelli's, Harry's New York Bar and the men's bar on the Cambon side of the Ritz were probably the three best known tippling Taj Mahals in the world and when every Atlantic liner set down hundreds of solvent and thirsty Yanks full of devaluated francs, Frank of the Ritz Bar was a sort of universally recognized king of saloonkeepers and was, in fact, a very pleasant, generous and understanding friend to thousands of Americans. There was nothing either cheap or popular about the Ritz and there was no dandruff on the morning jackets of its customers, who included Evander Berry Wall, the then King of Spain, the Prince of Wales, Phil Plant, William B. Leeds and the Russian Grand Dukes then living in exile in Paris. The men's bar was also the happy romping and stomping ground, in summer, of most of Harvard, Yale and Princeton with an occasional democratic leaven of Williams or Dartmouth.

The Sidecar was invented by Frank, so far as fallible human memory can determine, about 1923 as a sort of companion piece to the Stinger only with even more expensive ingredients. It was always built by Frank for favored customers with the Ritz's own bottling of a Vintage 1865 Cognac and set one back, in this redaction, the then equivalent of five American dollars.

*Sidecar:*     1¾ oz. brandy
¾ oz. cointreau
juice of half lime
*Shake and serve in 3 oz. cocktail glass.*

The Stinger, while enjoying a far more universal and less period-design vogue then the Sidecar, is probably the only drink which while properly a cocktail is also an after-dinner liqueur at the same time. Like the Sidecar it can be fashioned as a rich man's drink by the simple expedient of using fine vintage Cognac or as a more modest arrangement by the infusion in its economy of a California brandy. Except to the very exacting and financial taste, an entirely acceptable Stinger can be made if thoroughly chilled with Christian Brothers brandy.

**Stinger:**
1⅓ oz. brandy
1⅓ oz. white crème de menthe
*Shake and serve in 3 oz. cocktail glass.*

Ray Bolger is fond of a particular version of Scotch and soda to which he refers as a Bolger Over or Spooner Splash which requires the following ingredients:

**Bolger Over:**
2 oz. Scotch whisky
2 oz. club soda
1 inch Jack Spooner's thumb

The virtue of the drink, which must be served by Jack Spooner in person, lies in the flavor derived from his thumb in the glass, giving it a peculiar piquancy not available anywhere else.

From the Stork's own bar book come:

**Derby Cocktail:**
2 oz. gin
¾ oz. peach brandy
2 sprigs mint
*Shake well and serve in 3 oz. cocktail glass.*

**Habaneros:**
2 oz. Mexican rum
juice of half lime
4 dashes grenadine
*Shake and serve in 3 oz. cocktail glass.*

**Bermuda Rose:**

2 oz. gin
¾ oz. apricot brandy
2 dashes grenadine
*Shake and serve in 3 oz. cocktail glass.*


**Florida Cocktail:**

2 oz. rum
2 dashes green crème de menthe
juice of half lime
½ oz. pineapple juice
sugar to taste
*Shake, decorate with 2 sprigs of mint and
serve in Delmonico glass.*


**Santiago Cocktail:**

1¾ oz. rum
¾ oz. triple sec
1 tsp. sugar
juice of half lime
*Shake and serve in 3 oz. cocktail glass.*


**Army Cocktail:**

1½ oz. gin
1 oz. sweet vermouth
2 dashes grenadine
slice of orange peel
*Shake and serve in 3 oz. cocktail glass.*


**Ballet Russe Cocktail:** 2 oz. vodka
½ oz. crème de cassis
4 dashes lime juice
*Shake and serve in 3 oz. cocktail glass.*

**Bijou:**          1¼ oz. gin
                    ¾ oz. Chartreuse
                    ¾ oz. Italian vermouth
                    *Decorate with cherry. Twist of lemon peel*
                    *over drink. Stir and serve in 3 oz. cocktail*
                    *glass.*

Although of comparatively recent origin and evolution, the Zombie is a drink the precise source of which, like its exact economy, is subject to controversy. The author first encountered it as an aid to practical alcoholism in the celebrated premises of Trader Vic in Oakland, California, and almost immediately after that in a bamboo bar frequented by Hollywood script writers in search of inspiration to more than customary intellectual chaos. It may very well, as advertised, have been imported from far island places or it may just as plausibly have been the fevered brain child of Trader Vic himself, an opportunist whose ethics are unmuffled by any consideration of human well-being, but, whenever it came, the Zombie exploded into fullest flower at the New York World's Fair. It was the principal stock in trade of the Hurricane Bar in Flushing Meadows and was retailed one to a customer at a dollar a sample by a management at once thrifty and mindful of municipal ordinances. Actually it was not as lethal as advertised, but expediency will limit its consumption by the inexperienced, as the variety and proofs of the rums involved are both chancy elements in the human reckoning.

As will be apparent from the complexity of its ingredients, a Zombie is subject to multiple variations. This is the way Cookie can be persuaded to compound them for patrons with the most reassuring references:

**Zombian:**

1 oz. amber rum
1 oz. silver rum
1 oz. Jamaica rum
4 dashes cherry brandy
4 dashes apricot brandy
1 dash papaya juice
juice of half lime
*Serve in tall glass with cracked ice. Top with ½ oz. 151 proof rum. Stir. Decorate with green and red cherry and slice of orange. Serve with straws.*

Nobody seems ever with any impressive degree of persuasiveness to have been able to say just when such arrangements as a Zombie should be served (if ever) and present any logical reason why one time of day or night is any better (or worse) suited to their inhalation. True purists will scream that all mixed drinks save, perhaps, a vermouth cassis or gin and bitters are an abomination, and as such we have no concern with their cant. The fact stands that many people like many drinks at many times; some even going on record to the effect that they like all drinks at any time. The author of this book makes no attempt, save along the broadest of conceivable lines, to indicate the propriety of any given drink at any given time. The only person fit to be an arbiter in such matters is the consumer himself who will, in any case, drink just as he pleases in complete and magnificent disregard for what any authority in the matter may say. Anyhow, the author's Uncle Ned, who early in life absented himself from Framingham, Massachusetts, to live in Paris where he wore for many decades the same pearl gray derby and made astonishing sums of money playing roulette at the Banker's Club, believed the best time to drink an Haute Sauterne was at breakfast. The admission of this family solecism has always seemed an adequate excuse for the exemption of the author from jury duty in any matter of either gastronomic or sartorial taste.

Another clutch of restorative beverages, the individual items of which are more or less common currency just the other side of the red plush cord in Fifty-third Street are:

*Society Cocktail:*      1¾ oz. gin
                        ¾ oz. French vermouth
                        4 dashes grenadine
                        *Shake and serve in 3 oz. cocktail glass.*

*Applejack Cocktail:*    1½ oz. applejack
                        4 dashes grenadine
                        juice of half lemon
                        *Shake and serve in 3 oz. glass.*

*Frisco Cocktail:*       2 oz. bourbon
                        ¾ oz. benedictine
                        twist of lemon peel
                        *Stir and serve in 3 oz. cocktail glass.*

*Loch Lomond:*        2 oz. Scotch
                        2 dashes Angostura bitters
                        1 dash simple syrup
                        *Shake with shaved ice and serve in 3 oz. cocktail glass.*

*Scotch Rickey:*      1½ oz. Scotch
                        insert juice of half lime and rind in highball glass
                        1 cube ice
                        *Fill glass with seltzer and stir.*

| | |
|---|---|
| *Scotch "Cooler":* | 2 oz. Scotch<br>1 cube ice<br>peel rind of lemon in spiral form<br>1 split soda<br>*Serve in tall glass and stir.* |
| *Red Lion:* | 1½ oz. gin<br>¾ oz. grand marnier<br>3 dashes grenadine<br>¼ oz. lemon juice<br>*Shake and serve in 3 oz. cocktail glass.* |
| *Gin Buck:* | 2 oz. gin<br>juice of half lemon<br>2 cubes of ice<br>*Serve in tall glass, fill with ginger ale and stir.* |
| *Pink Lady:* | 1¾ oz. gin<br>½ oz. applejack<br>4 dashes grenadine<br>egg white<br>*Shake and serve in 4 oz. wine glass.* |
| *Star Cocktail:* | 1¾ oz. applejack<br>1 oz. Italian vermouth<br>*Stir and serve in 3 oz. cocktail glass.* |
| *Russian Cocktail:* | 1 oz. gin<br>1 oz. vodka<br>¾ oz. crème de cacao<br>*Shake and serve in 3 oz. cocktail glass.* |

**Pompier Highball (or Vermouth-Cassis):**

3 oz. French vermouth
4 dashes crème de cassis
seltzer
add lemon peel
*Serve in highball glass and stir.*

**Cooler:**

2 oz. gin
1 cube ice
peel rind of lemon in spiral form
1 split soda
*Serve in tall glass and stir.*

Most personal preferences in mixed drinks are simply variations on standard or basic themes in much the same manner that all witticisms are supposedly based on seven fundamental joke structures. Carole Landis, for example, swears by a vodka Martini which, if pursued over any length of time, she promises will make the customer scream next morning for a Bloody Mary.

**Vodka Martini #1:**

3 oz. vodka
1 oz. dry vermouth
*Stir or spoon with cube ice and serve as a conventional Martini in 4 oz. glass.*

**Bloody Mary:**

3 oz. vodka
6 oz. tomato juice
2 dashes Angostura bitters
juice of half lemon
*Shake these together with ice or mix in Waring mixer and serve cold in highball glass.*

Monty Woolley improves on the usual proportions of the dry Martini simply by increasing the conventional proportions of gin and vermouth to four to one, admonishes barkeeps to use cube ice and no lemon whatsoever, and, when asked what this will do for the consumer, remarks with a worldly leer: "Consult Lillian Russell!"

Still another variation on the theme of gin and vermouth, which Cole Porter in *The Two Little Babes in the Woods* discovered was the fountain of youth comes from Mary Astor:

### Astor Painless Anesthetic:

> 3 oz. gin
> 1 oz. French vermouth
> 1 oz. Italian vermouth
> 1 oz. cognac
> *Shake well with ice cubes and dash of orange bitters, twist of lemon peel and just a touch of sugar.*

Don Ameche frowns a masculine frown upon mixed liquor in any form on the understandable grounds that he is an admirer of straight bourbon whisky and no nonsense about a chaser. But Bonita Granville offers what she contends to be the barkeep's answer to the atomic bomb:

### Snow White:

> 5 oz. Southern Comfort
> 1 oz. vodka
> 1 oz. fresh pineapple juice
> ½ oz. orange juice
> *Mix in a Waring mixer and serve in an old-fashioned glass.*

A touch of sentiment attaches to the favorite drink of the ever-provocative Billie Burke Ziegfeld who writes in as follows:

"As I recall, a rather delightful drink Florenz Ziegfeld used to prepare was two-thirds gin and one-third pineapple juice, with the rim of the glass moistened in lemon juice or lime and then twirled in powdered sugar, served very cold. At least he always twirled the first two or three in powdered sugar. After that it didn't matter."

The sworn preference in mixed drinks of John Garfield, and he can be seen whenever in New York giving evidence in the Cub Room to support his testimony, is a Rob Roy or Scotch Manhattan, but Mischa Auer recommends an arrangement which he calls a "Balla-laika" and which, simply enough, depends for its authority on equal parts Cointreau, Vodka and orange juice frapped and served in a cocktail glass. Anne Jeffreys likes a conventional Golden Fizz but with the added attraction of grated cocoanut mixed in it, and Binnie Barnes goes to bat, literally, for a

| | |
|---|---|
| *Schnorkel:* | 2 oz. golden bacardi |
| | ½ oz. pernod |
| | juice of a large lime |
| | *Mix with a little sugar in a Waring mixer and, like the submarine for which the drink is named, you'll be submerged in no time and perhaps going backward to find out where you've been.* |

It is possible that long before the thirsty reader or patron as the case may be has exhausted this overwhelming catalogue of potables, or vice versa, the inner man or inner woman may be clamoring for solid nutriment and, whether they are served adjacent to the dance floor, in the Cub Room, the Blessed Events Room or elsewhere on the Stork premises, these are a few of the house specialties which make it difficult for Jinx Falkenberg to retain her figure:

### Filet Mignon Capucine:

Garnished with broiled stuffed mushrooms, creamed spinach, Bernaise Sauce.

### Guinea Hen:

Breast of Guinea Hen-Saute of garnished asparagus tips. New peas. Madeira Sauce.

### Tournedas Baltimore:

Small Tenderloin Saute with mushrooms smothered with onions. Sliced veal kidney, stewed tomatoes, German fried potatoes.

### Lamb Chop Saint Hilaire:

Lamb chop stuffed with chicken hash, garnished with sliced green pepper, stewed tomatoes.

### Minced Tenderloin of Beef a la Deutsch:

Sliced Tenderloin, garnished with green peppers. Tartlet of cream corn. Chateau Sauce.

### Pheasant Casserole Derby:

Roast Pheasant stuffed American style. Garnished with dried truffles and foie gras, Madeira Sauce.

### Royal Squab Knickerbocker:

Roast Royal Squab in casserole garnished with artichokes. Bottom Parisienne potatoes covered over with chopped hard boiled egg, bread crumbs, and parsley. Madeira Sauce.

### Squab of Guinea Hen—Steve Hannagan

Squab of Guinea Hen, split and saute in butter, garnished with sliced oranges, black cherries. Porto Sauce.

### Broiled Chop of Venaison Ground Veneur:

Broiled chop of Venaison garnished with purée of chestnut, Sauce of Poivrade and currant jelly.

### Aiguilette of Duckling Florida:

Aiguilette of duckling in top of crouton of hominy, garnished with stewed pears, oranges and apples and pineapple. Porto Sauce.

### Minute Steak Chez Toi:

Steak Saute, garnished with diced potatoes, small glacé onions and mushrooms.

### Breast of Chicken Rimini:

Breast of chicken-Pique with truffle—serve in crustade. Purée of mushrooms. Supreme Sauce.

### Squab Chicken Louisiane:

Fried Squab chicken breaded. Garnish with sweet fried potatoes, stewed corn, fried bananas Rue Pilaw, Maryland Sauce.

As has been remarked elsewhere in this handbook for eatalls and tosspots of the Fifty-third Street persuasion, nobody in the world drinks all the drinks herein recorded, which is one of God's major mercies, and very few people drink very many of them, but somebody drinks every one of them and what has merit in the sight of any single individual, particularly if he is a notable of this world, is worth passing on for the amusement or instruction of his contemporaries.

Of the several hundred Stork celebrities canvassed in this poll of the flagon-conscious, an overwhelmingly large proportion recorded their preferences as being anything but exotic. Straight bourbon whisky, Scotch and soda, Martini and old-fashioned cocktails predominated on approximately a ten to one basis. A list of the top-drawer names which will vote any time for gin and vermouth against all the confections of all the Harry's New York Bars, Hurricane Bars, Palace Hotels, Ritz Hotels, Gardens of Allah, Pump Rooms and Alibi Bars of the world would stretch from Fifth Avenue to the County Strip, Los Angeles, and would read like an editorial synthesis of *Who's Who, Burke's Peerage,* the *International Motion Picture Almanac,* the *Directory of Directors* and the Palm Beach telephone directory.

Then, too, there are old accustomed patrons of Sherman's Shack whose taste for more unusual drinks still follows the conventional bar recipes like Jack Benny, who is a fall guy for Bloody Marys, Ruth Hussey, who dotes on Sazaracs, and Nanette Fabry, who confesses she can take and can't leave Southern Comforts.

Jinx Falkenberg, however, comes up with a Sangrita which she claims is a "favorite with bullfighters in Mexico and me," which is a not too distant relative of claret lemonade:

| | |
|---|---|
| ***Sangrita:*** | 2 oz. claret |
| | ½ oz. pineapple juice |
| | 6 oz. soda |
| | ½ oz. lime juice |
| | *Mix as a highball, preferably in a tall blue glass like those used at Cesar's Cafe in Tia Juana. Really a temperance drink.* |

Lilian Harvey likes:

| | |
|---|---|
| ***Hocus-Pocus:*** | 2 oz. gin |
| | 2 oz. cointreau |
| | 2 oz. lemon juice |
| | *Frappe and serve in a champagne glass.* |

James Gleason suggests a nonesuch known as a "Help Wanted Cocktail" comprising equal parts bourbon whisky and apricot brandy, shaken up with a few drops of lemon juice added and adds that in bed is a good place to try it if one has more than three.

Judy Canova, if pressed, will tell you that she likes:

**Pink Goody:**    1 oz. gin
         1 oz. golden bacardi
         1 oz. lime juice
         Dash of maraschino or grenadine
         *Serve with crushed ice in a tall highball glass with a generous splash of soda and a stick of pineapple for garnish. After the first drink, she submits, the fruit decoration may be eliminated as unessential.*

Andrea King, who confesses that, to date, she has only dared use the formula in half portions and then on an isolated atoll in the South Pacific, recommends:

**Devil's Tail:**    3 oz. 151 proof Rum
         3 oz. vodka
         1 oz. lime juice
         2 oz. grenadine
         *To obtain the best results, says Miss King, these should be frapped in a Waring mixer and served with a float of apricot brandy on top.*

Gertrude Niesen asserts that, when thirsty, she does hone and hanker for a conservative little toddy she has dreamed up called a

**Niesen Buzz-Bomb:**
1 oz. lime juice
1 oz. cointreau
1 oz. cognac
1 oz. benedictine
1 oz. vodka
*Shake well with crushed ice, strain into a tall highball glass and serve with a fill-up of the best vintage champagne.*

Arthur Berry cannot resist:

**Rum Bana:**
3 oz. Jamaica rum
1 oz. lemon juice
1 tsp. sugar
1 peeled banana
*Frappe in a Waring mixer and serve in a broad, flat champagne glass.*

And now a few more of the Stork Club's own bar list before we close the bar and retire to the Cub Room for the night.

**Barbary Cocktail:**
¾ oz. Scotch
¾ oz. gin
¾ oz. crème de cacao
½ oz. fresh cream
*Shake with shaved ice and serve in Delmonico glass.*

**East India Cocktail:**
1½ oz. brandy
¾ oz. pineapple juice
½ oz. orange curaçao
*Decorate with cherry, shake and serve in 3 oz. cocktail glass.*

**Honeymoon:**

1½ oz. applejack
½ oz. benedictine
juice of half lemon
3 dashes curaçao
*Shake and serve in 3 oz. cocktail glass.*

**Hawaii Cocktail:**

1½ oz. gin
1 oz. pineapple juice
1 dash orange bitters
white of egg
*Shake and serve in 4 oz. wine glass.*

**Coronation Cocktail:**

1½ oz. sherry
1 oz. French vermouth
2 dashes maraschino
3 dashes orange bitters
*Stir and serve in a 3 oz. glass.*

**Ojen Cocktail:**

2 oz. Ojen
1 dash Peychaud bitters
1 tsp. sugar
½ oz. water
*Shake and serve in 3 oz. cocktail glass.*

**Merry Widow:**

1⅓ oz. gin
1⅓ oz. dubonnet
*Twist of lemon peel. Stir and serve in 3 oz. cocktail glass.*

**Shandygaff:**

cold beer
cold ginger ale
*No ice. Serve in tall glass.*

**Lorraine Cocktail:**

1¾ oz. kirsch
½ oz. benedictine
juice of half lime
*Shake and serve in 3 oz. cocktail glass.*

**Kangaroo Kicker:**

2 oz. vodka
¾ oz. French vermouth
*Shake. Twist of lemon peel on top. Serve in 3 oz. cocktail glass.*

**Armour Cocktail:**

1¾ oz. dry sherry
1 oz. sweet vermouth
twist of lemon peel
*Stir and serve in 3 oz. cocktail glass.*

**R.A.F. Cocktail:**

1¾ oz. applejack
¾ oz. apricot brandy
juice of half lemon
*Shake and serve in 3 oz. cocktail glass.*

**Opal Cocktail:**

2 oz. absinthe
½ oz. yellow chartreuse
¼ oz. water
*Stir and serve in 4 oz. wine glass.*

**Napoleon:**

2 oz. gin
2 dashes dubonnet
2 dashes curaçao
2 dashes Fernet Branca
*Squeeze lemon peel on top. Shake and serve in 4 oz. wine glass.*

| | |
|---|---|
| *Americano Highball:* | 1 oz. Campari bitters<br>2 oz. sweet vermouth<br>*Serve in highball glass. Twist of lemon peel.*<br>*Top with seltzer and stir.* |
| *Spritzer Highball:* | *Pour 3 oz. chilled Rhine wine in highball glass. One cube of ice. Fill with chilled seltzer.* |
| *Alaska Cocktail:* | 2 oz. gin<br>¾ oz. yellow chartreuse<br>*Stir and serve in 3 oz. cocktail glass.* |
| *Moscow Mule:* | 2 oz. vodka<br>1 split ginger beer<br>crushed ice<br>*Serve in mug and decorate with sprigs of mint.* |

This volume pretends in no way to the dimensions or erudition of a cellar book. It is a bar book and as such concerns itself with the simple and essentially naive drinking habits of people in search of comfort, refreshment and the uses of pleasant company rather than the researches of oenophiles and the crafty cellar practices of learned wine stewards.

Ten bottles of champagne are served at the Stork to every one of claret, Burgundy, sauterne or Rhenish for the obvious reason that the pleasures of champagne are immediate to every perceptive sense and that it is a for-fun wine. George Saintsbury might not approve the drinking practices of the Cub Room but he would most assuredly have a good time following them. Mrs. Stuyvesant Fish quite literally floated her way into a reigning position in the New York society of the century's turn by the serving of Niagaras of the very best sparkling wine and other people have done it since. It was Mamie Fish who abolished at her dinners as a tiresome bore the classic service of a variety of wines, each appropriate to its proper course, and served nothing but champagne from soup to dessert with the result that her guests often got to Opera before the end of the second act, an innovation which rocked society to its foundations.

There is no food or time of the day and night when the service and consumption of champagne is not both appropriate and agreeable, a circumstance which attaches to no other beverage yet devised by vintners, brewers or distillers. With the close of hostilities in Europe the products of the great established champagne firms of Rheims and Epernay are again almost universally available in the brands always popular in the United States and England: Bollinger, Veuve Clicquot, Mumm's, Perrier Jouet, Krug, Charles Heidsick, Louis Roederer, Moet and Chandon, Lanson, and a few others of the first importance. The vintages of '33 and '37 will undoubtedly dominate the market for many years to come, but connoisseurs, knowing that wine of vintage quality often is bottled as an undated wine to protect the market, is never impressed by a vintage wine of second quality when he finds on the card such numbers as Krug's Private Cuvee, Bollinger Brut or Perrier-Jouet Dry England. The sans annee wine is often a very superior product indeed with the added inducement that it is usually a couple of dollars cheaper than the vintage years whose prices are jealously and zealously maintained at high levels by shippers, dealers and restaurateurs alike.

Aside from champagnes, New York's taste in table wines runs almost exclusively to claret and Burgundy and the German wines of the Rhine. Bordeaux (claret) generally is regarded as less pretentious than the classic vintages of Burgundy, and white Bordeaux or sauternes enjoy a certain vogue with the service of fish and luncheon dishes of a light nature. True Chablis, the aristocrat of white still wines, is so difficult to obtain as this is being written as to be inconsiderable in this brief footnote.

Since discussions of the merits, qualities and service of even one of the classes of wine mentioned have over several centuries engaged the attentions of many learned men and have supplied the matter for innumerable and ponderous books, it will be seen that any detailed mention of them, let alone so chancy a subject as an estimate of current vintages, is impracticable in the extreme, as well as outside the province of this book.

As has been the case with the vintages of the grape, it is not the purpose of this bar book to trespass upon the provinces which are more properly those of a cellar book, and brandies in all their redactions, classifications and varieties of wonder are more properly the concerns of a sommelier than of a barkeep. With the exceptions of a few formulas, they are unsuited to use in mixed drinks, being an essence for the consideration of the mature palate and the discretion of experience. Brandy is the drink for heroes and it is also the drink for scholars. Even the brashest barkeep hesitates at the command of a patron for a pedigreed Cognac to be used in a stinger or rendered in highball form with soda water.

Many and learned books have been devoted to Cognac and its allied or related eaux de vie and the Stork stocks a supply that is the wonder and pleasure of the knowing and the undoing of the unjudicious, for a great Cognac has about it a pantherlike treachery in that its absorption seems quite devoid of dismaying results until next day or even next week. It possesses, too, the humorous attribute of deluding the consumer into the belief that he is entirely sober until he finds himself, like David Copperfield at his first wine dinner, unaccountably face down on the stair landing and enquiring of kind friends who it might have been that has so rudely fallen.

Only research and a considerable investment of time and patience can fairly determine an individual taste in Cognacs and the experts will dispute the matter until Judgment Day. Its frequently low alcoholic content should never be taken as an index of its chemical and toxic strength and some of the most perilous of all Fines of great age may be no more than thirty-six or forty percent alcohol. Personally the taste of the author runs to a Cognac or Fine Champagne approximately forty years old, an age when the brands and blends of all accredited houses are possessed of common and often indistinguishable qualities of even mellowness without too great a strain on their essential strength and vitality. In common practice the stars on Cognac should indicate approximately three years of age.

The initials by which Cognacs are classified vary with different firms of export but, again, generally speaking, they may be interpreted as follows:

E: Especial
F: Fine
V: Very
O: Old
S: Superior
P: Pale
X: Extra
C: Cognac

Thus it will be seen that a VSOP is, within the honor of the distiller and his established reputation for an honest description of his product, a Very Superior Old Pale Cognac, but none of these adjectives has any formal definition or meaning beyond the discretion of the firm which uses it. In the realm of commercial Cognacs the names Hennessy, Hines, Denis Mounier and a few others are more to be trusted than many stars and all the initials which customarily follow the names of British admirals.

The entire matter of after dinner liqueurs resolves itself into one of personal taste and preference and neither advice nor instructions in their use seem altogether valid. The sweet, highly aromatic cordial, generally speaking, is a survival of a more florid and rococo age of drinking and manners, and their use in the United States at the moment is almost entirely confined to infusion in mixed drinks, but it doesn't take any graybeard to recall a period when they were held in high and universal esteem and their service in elaborate profusion was a hallmark of gentility and sophistication.

The trans-Atlantic liners of twenty-five years ago were probably the last great stronghold of the liqueur. At the same time no dinner in London or Paris was complete without the appearance of an almost overwhelming variety of sweet cordials with flavors deriving from every known flower and herb and a few unheard of by anyone: Benedictine, Chartreuse, Cointreau, Kümmel, Curaçao, Triple Sec, Crème de Cacao, Crème de Cassis, Maraschino, Prunella, Peach Brandy, Grand Marnier, Danziger Goldwasser, Flora Delle Alpi, Kirsch, Drambuie, Anise and Swedish Punch. They came in every variety of bottle, tall, squat and flattened, globular, square, octagonal, fluted, beribboned, chaste and plain, austere and fanciful.

Today the run of liqueurs has subsided almost to the vanishing point although a green or white mint frappe or glass of Cointreau is occasionally seen.

Nine Americans out of ten who do not order a highball after dinner call for Cognac, American brandy, Armagnac or one of the related eaux de vie of the family of grape spirits.

It is with the greatest infrequency, nowadays, that private drinking parties or groups of night club guests of modest size command the preparation of the elaborate communal punches, grogs, eggnogs and sangarees which a century ago were the staples in all public taverns and ordinaries. Large quantities of punch are still in vogue for weddings, receptions and other formal occasions where their purpose is partly as refreshment, partly for ornament and the sake of tradition. The punchbowl as such has largely disappeared from public bars, although the author can well remember when an enormous bath of Adams House Punch was set out every morning on the bar of that once wonderful hotel in Boston and was a day-long favorite with tarriers at the Washington Street entry of Calvin Coolidge's favorite hotel.

These more or less elaborate drinks, most of which have one variety of rum or another for the base, are, however, still popular in individual service and the closer one gets to the tropics the more frequently one encounters such standards of hot country drinking as Planter's Punch, Fish House Punch, rum swizzle and gin coolers. The most celebrated of all American regional drinks, the Mint Julep, is, in actual fact, a highly concentrated individual serving of Bourbon Whisky Punch.

Of the several score punches in the bright and heady lexicon of the Stork Club the following are the elaborate mixed drinks most in requisition in the ordinary course of the seasons:

***Roman Punch:***

1 tsp. sugar
juice of half lemon
juice of half orange
white of egg, beaten
2 oz. rum
*Shake well. Fill goblet with chilled champagne.*

**Claret Punch:**

3 oz. claret
juice of half lemon
2 dashes curaçao
1 tsp. sugar
*Dress with fruit and serve in goblet with fine ice, squirt of seltzer.*

**Brandy Punch:**

2 oz. brandy
sugar to taste
1 dash grenadine
1 dash maraschino
shaved ice
*Use goblet. Dress with mint and fruit. Stir well. Squirt of seltzer.*

**Sauterne Punch:**

(for 1 gallon)
juice of five lemons
2 ponies brandy
1 pony applejack
1½ oz. pineapple juice
2 dashes yellow chartreuse
2 qt. sauterne
2 qt. sparkling water
*Sugar to taste. Cucumber rinds. Dress with fruit.*

**Pimm's #1:**

2 cubes of ice
slice of lemon
cucumber rind
lemon soda
2 oz. Pimm's No. 1
*Serve in tall glass and stir.*

**Whisky Punch:**

2 oz. whisky
juice of half lemon
1 tsp. sugar
shaved ice
*Use goblet. Dress with fruit. Squirt of seltzer.*

**Brandy Rickey:**

1½ oz. brandy
juice of half lime and rind
1 cube ice
*Stir and serve in highball glass. Fill glass with seltzer.*

**Crustas:**

2 oz. Jamaica rum
juice of one lime
½ tsp. sugar
3 dashes maraschino
2 dashes Angostura bitters
*Shake. Sugar rim of glass. Peel of half orange in Tom Collins glass. Cracked ice to the top and fill with soda. Decorate with fruit and serve with straws.*

**Pousse-Cafe:**

⅛ oz. grenadine (red color)
⅛ oz. crème de cacao (black color)
⅛ oz. maraschino (white color)
⅛ oz. orange curaçao (orange color)
⅛ oz. crème Yvette (violet color)
⅛ oz. brandy (amber color)
*Pour in the order named very carefully and slowly in cordial glasses to prevent cloudiness.*

| | |
|---|---|
| *Peach Velvet:* | insert raw peach in peach champagne glass<br>fill with chilled champagne<br>1 dash peach brandy on top |
| *Rum Cobbler:* | 2 oz. rum<br>2 dashes lemon juice<br>1 tsp. sugar<br>dash of cherry brandy<br>*Shake and decorate with fruit, sprig of mint.* |
| *Rum Punch:* | juice of half lemon<br>1 tsp. sugar<br>2 oz. rum<br>1 dash brandy<br>*Fruit. Serve in goblet with fine ice.* |
| *Clog-Hot Wine Drink:* | ¾ cup sugar<br>2 oz. Angostura bitters<br>1 pint sherry wine<br>1 pint claret wine<br>½ pint brandy<br>*Use large flame proof casserole. Place over fire until piping hot. Serve in old-fashioned glass or mug. (Serves fifteen.)* |

In the Stork Club's repertory of more exotic drinks and one which calls for some special notice because of its antecedents and background is certainly the Blue Blazer. As in the cases of the Sidecar and the Gibson, the originator of the Blue Blazer is known to the record, and historical research has disclosed that the arrangement in all its Paine's Fireworks splendor was first produced—perhaps detonated would be a better word—by Professor Jerry Thomas, a celebrated barkeep of the last century, while working at the El Dorado, a San Francisco oasis of wide repute, in 1849.

Professor Thomas, who stemmed from New Haven, where he had practiced since early manhood on the nearly impregnable persons of Yale undergraduates, was famous as a practitioner who could gentle the most voracious drinker fresh from the placer diggings of Hangtown, and one evening his talents were put to the ultimate test. A whiskered giant, booted to the hips and clattering with Colt's patent firearms, demanded satisfaction. "Fix me," he roared, "some hell-fire that will shake me right down to my gizzard."

Professor Thomas consulted his files, his assistants, and then, while the word spread throughout Geary Street that great doings were afoot and crowds gathered, he prepared to do his stuff. First he set upon the bar (according to Herbert Asbury, the learned historian of Americana) the two silver mugs, imported from New York around the Horn, that were the show utensils of the El Dorado.

"Gentlemen," he announced. "You are about to witness the birth of a new beverage!"

"A sigh of anticipation arose from the assemblage," writes Mr. Asbury in recording the occasion, "and with one accord the mass of men moved forward until they stood, respectfully, five deep before the bar, the whiskered giant, still booted, in the front rank. Professor Thomas smiled and quietly poured a tumbler of Scotch whisky into one of the mugs, followed by a slightly smaller quantity of boiling water. Then with an evil smelling sulphur match, he ignited the liquid and, as the blue flame shot toward the ceiling and the crowd fell back in awe, he hurled the blazing mixture back and forth between the two mugs, with a rapidity and dexterity that was well nigh unbelievable. This amazing spectacle continued in full movement for perhaps ten seconds, and then Professor Thomas poured the beverage into a tumbler and smothered the flame. He stirred a spoonful of pulverized white sugar into the mixture, added a twist of lemon peel, and shoved the smoking concoction across to the booted and spurred giant.

" 'Sir,' said Professor Thomas, bowing, 'The Blue Blazer!'

"The boastful miner threw back his head and flung the boiling drink down his throat. He stood motionless for a moment, smacking his lips and tasting the full flavor of it, and then a startled expression spread over his face. He swayed like a reed in the wind. He shivered from head to foot. His teeth rattled. He batted his eyes. His mouth opened and closed; he could say nothing. Then he sank slowly into a chair. He was no longer fit to be tied."*

*Blue Blazer:*

1 wine glass Scotch whisky
1 wine glass boiling water
*Use two large silver-plated mugs with handles. Put the whisky into one mug and the boiling water into the other, ignite the whisky with fire, and while blazing mix both ingredients by pouring them four or five times from one mug to the other. If well done this will have the appearance of a continued stream of liquid fire. Sweeten with powdered sugar and serve in a small bar tumbler with a piece of lemon peel.*

While possessed of neither the spectacular nor the fire hazard qualities of the masterpiece devised by Professor Thomas, there are several other arrangements dependent upon the skill and artistry of the barkeep or cellarman for their effectiveness rather than their alcoholic content alone:

*From The Bon Vivant's Companion, edited by Herbert Asbury, ©1927, 1928 by Alfred A. Knopf, Inc. and reprinted by permission of the publishers.*

**Brandy Caprice:**  *Make an incision around center of orange. Carefully pull skin back towards one end so as to form a cup and still be fastened to orange. Pour ½ oz. of brandy and ignite. While burning, slowly pass one lump of sugar in a teaspoon through flame until sugar melts. Stir.*

**Tom and Jerry:**  1 whole egg
1 tsp. sugar
1½ oz. Jamaica rum
*Beat up yolk and white of egg separately. Then mix the yolk and white together. Use stem glass or China mug, adding the spirits, then, fill with boiling water. Dash of brandy. Top with nutmeg. Serve in Tom & Jerry mug.*

**Major Bailey:**  2 oz. gin
4 dashes lemon juice
1 tsp. sugar
crushed mint
shaved ice
*Serve in silver mug or tall glass. Stir very well until mug is frosted. Decorate with sprigs of mint and serve with straws.*

**Singapore Sling:**  2 oz. gin
¾ oz. cherry brandy
1 dash benedictine
juice of lemon
*Serve in tall glass with 2 cubes of ice. Decorate with slice of orange and sprig of mint. Top with carbonic.*

**Cafe Au Kirsch:**

1½ oz. kirsch
1 tsp. sugar
white of egg
add coffee
*Shake and serve in wine glass.*

**After-Dinner Cocktail:**

1 oz. prunella brandy
1 oz. cherry brandy
dash lemon juice
*Shake and serve in 4 oz. wine glass.*

**B and B:**

½ oz. benedictine
½ oz. brandy
*Serve in cordial glass.*

**Tropical Cocktail:**

¾ oz. crème de cacao
1¼ oz. French vermouth
¾ oz. maraschino
1 dash orange bitters
*Shake well and serve in 4 oz. wine glass.*

**Champagne Punch (for 1 gallon):**

2 qt. champagne
1 pony maraschino
3 ponies brandy
1 pony curaçao
1 dash yellow chartreuse
juice of four lemons
2 qt. sparkling water
sugar to taste
fruit
block of ice

**Rocky Mountain Cooler:**

1 egg
1 tsp. simple syrup
4 dashes Angostura bitters
juice of one lemon
6 oz. cider
*Put ingredients into shaker, add cracked ice sufficient and shake thoroughly. Strain into 10 oz. glass. Dust with nutmeg, serve with straws.*

**Zoom:**

1½ oz. brandy
¼ oz. honey
½ oz. fresh cream
*Shake and serve in 4 oz. wine glass.*

**Hot Buttered Rum:**

1½ oz. Jamaica rum
1 lump sugar
1 small slice butter
4 cloves
*Use an old-fashioned glass or mug. Fill with boiling water. Stir.*

**Sangaree:**

3 oz. port or sherry wine
1 tsp. sugar
cracked ice
slice of lemon
*Fill glass with water. Serve in Tom Collins glass. Nutmeg on top. Stir.*

Which brings us inevitably to the controversial and endlessly embattled subject of what, for all its association in the popular imagination with the south and southern chivalry, is probably the nearest thing extant to the American national drink, the classic of classics, the colonel's delight, a snare and engine of destruction for the unwary, the ever changing yet immutable and changeless mint julep.

The fallacious belief that adequate juleps cannot be served, obtained or appreciated anywhere north of, at the very extremity of geographic possibility, Baltimore, has long since vanished in the face of overwhelming evidence to the contrary. The julep can and does flourish, green-bay-tree like, within the boundaries of Manhattan and, more specifically and even more handily for present purposes, in Fifty-third Street not a seltzer squirt from Fifth Avenue.

Space, the informed intelligence of the author and the patience of thirsty readers all militate against any prolonged discussion of the several and various aspects of juleps. The author has hoisted them gratefully in silver chalices of half quart capacity in Maysville, Kentucky, overlooking the incomparable vista of the Ohio as the Chesapeake and Ohio's "George Washington" has rolled down the valley at summer dusk. He has lifted them in the perfumed precincts of a springtime garden in Charleston in little gold toddy mugs that were prized in the family still owning them when gentlemen wore court swords on the street and satin breeches and silver buckled pumps were taken for granted. He has drunk drastic juleps in Natchez-Above-the-Levee that made him wonder how the Mississippi packet gamblers of the fifties with their skirted coats and the Remington derringers concealed in lace cuffs could see a hand of cards. And he has accepted juleps that were a sacrament in old walled gardens in New Orleans while the sailors fought fistfights and the town tarts paraded the ill-lit and uneven pavements of Royal Street nearby.

All the juleps were good. Some seemed better than others, but that was only because the others had been drunk first.

Let, as in the *Rubaiyat*, the "four and seventy jarring sects" dispute the merits of crushed ice and shaved ice, of pounded mint, muddled mint and only bruised mint (adjectives which so often lend themselves equally handily to the julep drinkers themselves) and the virtue of just a small slug of overproof Jamaica rum floating on top of the whole creation. This is the Stork julep and it has stayed and strengthened many brave men and fair women, confirming them in the almost irrefutable belief that most of the good things of the world come in glass bottles and that the very best of them say bourbon on the outside:

**Mint Julep:**          2 oz. bourbon
                         1 tsp. sugar
                         4 sprigs mint
                         *Mash with muddler. Fill the silver mug with*
                         *shaved ice. Stir until the outside of the mug*
                         *is frosted. Decorate with sprigs of mint and*
                         *serve with straws. Add green cherry.*

Personally, the author cleaves to a slight variance of the foregoing: four ounces of Jack Daniel's proof bourbon with a float of two ounces of Hines' Triomph Cognac on top.

Officer, please back the patrol wagon nearer the curb; the step is too high for my mother.

An appendix of Drinks

suggested by members of the

staff of the Stork Club . . .

**A**nyone who peruses the content of this bar book will discover that, integrated in its editorial economy, are a number of drink suggestions and recipes originating with patrons of the Stork and differing in more or less degree from the nearest related and established drink. As the devising of new and more fascinating ways of insinuating alcohol and the pleasant humors that accompany its proper absorption into the human system is by no means confined to guests, it was thought by the author a shrewd notion to solicit some recipes by members of the staff.

The gustatory ruffles and flourishes in this appendix are the brain children of various members of Mr. Billingsley's staff, and they are included as evidence of its versatility in the practice of the useful arts and sciences.

Most of them originate with Nathaniel Cook, the chief barman, but almost everyone, from Eddie Whittmer and Harry Kaye, the captains, to Veronica Harrold, who holds hats prettily for ransom at the door, wanted in, and here are their contributions to the practical humanities.

Cookie's secret archives contain the following:

*Spiker Cocktail:*    ⅓ oz. green crème de menthe
⅔ oz. imported brandy
*Serve in 3 oz. cocktail glass, well chilled.*
*Shake well and strain.*

**Stork Club Cooler:**

1 tsp. sugar
juice of half orange
2 oz. gin
*Serve in 12 oz. Collins glass and shake well and strain into glass with shaved ice and serve decorated with fruit and straws.*

**Eye-Opener:**

1 oz. pineapple juice
dash maraschino
1½ oz. brandy
*Shake and strain. Serve in 3 oz. cocktail glass.*

**Bourbon Society:**

1 oz. bourbon
*Serve in an old-fashioned glass with 6 or 8 tiny ice cubes and a twist of dropped lemon peel.*

**F.B.I. Fizz:**

½ oz. Cherry Heering brandy
½ oz. bourbon
½ oz. Jamaica rum
twist orange peel
*Serve in 8 oz. highball glass. Shake well and strain into glass with two ice cubes and top with soda water.*

**Detroit Daisy:**

dash grenadine
juice of one lime
2 oz. rum (dark)
add fresh mint leaves
*Serve in 12 oz. Collins glass. Shake hard. Strain into glass filled with shaved ice. Decorate with sprig of mint and green cherry.*

**Blinker Cocktail:**     dash grenadine
¾ oz. grapefruit juice
1½ oz. rye whisky
*Shake well and strain. Serve in 3 oz. cocktail glass.*

Arthur Berry, a captain of waiters, donates the specifications for:

**Kicking Cow:**     ⅓ oz. maple syrup
⅓ cream
⅔ oz. bourbon or rye
*Shake well and use cracked ice. Serve in a cocktail glass.*

And the following are the dream children of Eddie Whittmer:

**Edith Day Cocktail:**     white of one egg
¾ jigger of grapefruit juice
1 jigger of dry gin
½ tsp. sugar
*Serve in a champagne glass, well frapped.*

**Wildflower Cocktail:**     1 dash of grenadine
¾ jigger grapefruit juice
1 jigger of Scotch whisky
*Serve in a hollow stem champagne glass, well frapped.*

**Blessed Event:**     juice of half lime
dash of curaçao
2 oz. benedictine
2 oz. applejack
*Shake and strain. Serve in cocktail glass.*

**Brooklynite:**

dash of lime juice
½ oz. of honey
2 oz. Jamaica rum
dash of Angostura bitters
*Shake well and strain. Serve in 3 oz. cocktail glass.*

**Stork Club Cocktail:**

dash of lime juice
juice of half orange
dash of triple sec
1½ oz. gin
dash of Angostura bitters
*Shake well and strain in chilled 4 oz. glass.*

**Salty Dog Collins:**

juice of one lime
¼ tsp. salt
1½ oz. gin
*Shake in a cocktail shaker and pour into 10 oz. glass with two ice cubes.*

**Cuff and Buttons:**

juice of half lime
4 dashes of sweet vermouth
2 oz. Southern Comfort
*Shake in a cocktail shaker, strain and serve chilled in 3 oz. glass.*

**4th Estate Cocktail:**

⅓ oz. French vermouth
⅓ oz. Italian vermouth
⅓ oz. gin
4 dashes absinthe
*Stir well and strain into 3 oz. cocktail glass. Add cherry and twist lemon peel.*

**Debutante's Dream:**    ⅓ oz. bourbon
⅓ oz. brandy
⅓ oz. orange juice
dash of lemon juice
*Shake well and strain. Serve in 3 oz. cocktail glass.*

**Mr. New Yorker:**    1¾ oz. French vermouth
½ oz. gin
½ oz. dry sherry
dash of cointreau
*Stir and strain. Serve in 3 oz. cocktail glass.*

**Queens Taste Cocktail:** ⅓ oz. French vermouth
⅔ oz. gin
few leaves of fresh crushed mint
*Stir and strain. Serve in chilled 3 oz. cocktail glass.*

**Orchid Cocktail:**    dash crème Yvette
white of one egg
2 oz. gin
*Serve in chilled 4 oz. wine glass. Shake hard and strain. Use only a dash of crème Yvette. It will produce a delightful violet flavor, with a coloring as nice as an orchid flower.*

**A Dream Cocktail:**    dash of triple sec
dash of lime juice
dash cream
1½ oz. gin
*Shake and strain. Serve in 3 oz. cocktail glass.*

Albert Coleman, one of Cookie's vicars at the bar has evolved:

**Wally Cocktail:**
⅓ oz. lime juice
⅓ oz. peach brandy
⅓ oz. applejack
*Shake well. Serve in a cocktail glass.*

**Golden Slipper:**
1 pony of yellow chartreuse
1 yolk of egg
1 pony of goldwasser
*Pour one pony of yellow chartreuse into sherry glass. Then drop yolk of egg without breaking it and then add one pony of goldwasser on top.*

**Yellow Parrot:**
⅓ oz. absinthe
½ oz. yellow chartreuse
⅓ oz. apricot brandy
*Shake well. Serve in a cocktail glass.*

**Zaranes Cocktail:**
½ oz. vodka
½ oz. apricot brandy
dash of Angostura bitters
*Shake well. Serve in a cocktail glass.*

**Brandy Smash:**
½ tsp. sugar
1 squirt of seltzer
4 sprigs of mint
1 wine glass of brandy
*Serve in a champagne glass. Fill with fine ice, stir well with a spoon. Press the mint to extract the essence as in a julep. Decorate with berries or fruit.*

**Daily Double C:**     1 oz. rum
1 oz. Italian vermouth
2 cherries
*Mix with ice and stir. Serve in a cocktail glass.*

From Julius Corsani, barman, come the "Julius Special" and "Rum Scoundrel":

**Julius Special:**     ⅓ oz. lime juice
⅓ oz. cointreau
⅔ oz. Jamaica rum—3 Daggers
*Serve in a cocktail glass.*

**Rum Scoundrel:**     ⅓ oz. lime juice
⅔ oz. white or gold bacardi rum
1 tsp. sugar
*Serve in an old-fashioned glass. Rub the edge of the glass with lemon and dip in sugar to coat it.*

The nominations of Donald Arden, chief of Mr. Billingsley's staff of publicists, are:

**Golden Panther (for three):**
2 oz. gin
2 oz. brandy
2 oz. whisky
1 oz. dry vermouth
juice of half orange
*Serve in 6 oz. glass. Pour ingredients into a shaker with cracked ice. Shake well and pour into individual glasses.*

### All American Punch (30 persons):

15 oz. Southern Comfort
5 bottles Coca Cola
3 6-oz. bottles soda
1 oz. cherry juice
5 oranges
3 lemons
2 limes
12 cherries

*Dice cherries into small pieces and squeeze the oranges and lemons and limes. Pour into punch bowl and add Coca Cola, soda, cherry juice, and Southern Comfort. Add shaven and crushed ice to chill thoroughly. Stir until chilled. Serve in a chilled punch glass.*

According to the sworn testimony of Joe Acre, captain, the vodka Martini is a favorite with Dashiel Hammett:

### Vodka Martini #2:

⅓ oz. French vermouth
⅔ oz. vodka

*Serve in a cocktail glass. Serve very cold.*

While Leo Spitzel, captain, asserts that a "Stratosphere Cocktail" will do wonders for you:

### Stratosphere Cocktail:

glass of champagne
¾ oz. crème Yvette

*Serve in a champagne glass. Add a few dashes of crême Yvette to champagne until purple colored. Add two pieces of clove and serve very cold.*

Frank Harris, the door captain, favors a "Franko-Ra":

**Franko-Ra:**

1 oz. white bacardi
⅔ oz. orange juice
⅓ oz. lemon juice
tsp. of sugar
*Shake well. Serve in a cocktail glass.*

Edward G. Johnson, a captain, urges customers on to a "Frozen Strawberry Daiquiri":

**Frozen Strawberry Daiquiri:**

1½ oz. Daiquiri rum
1½ oz. lemon juice
3 or 4 ripe strawberries
small spoonful of sugar
*Serve in a champagne glass. Make in the same manner as the usual frozen Daiquiri in the Waring mixer. It should come out with a nice color.*

While Arnold Sanchez, of the bar staff, assails the Gringo palates with a "South of the Border":

**South of the Border Longtail:**

1 oz. Southern Comfort
6 oz. milk
½ tsp. sugar
1 banana
nutmeg
*Serve in a Tom Collins glass. Put ingredients in a frozen Daiquiri mixer with little shaved ice for one minute.*

And Ernest Luthi, captain, recommends a "French Daiquiri":

**French Daiquiri:**          ½ oz. lime juice
                              ⅔ oz. bacardi rum
                              a little sugar
                              dash of cassis
                              few fresh mint leaves
                              *Shake well. Serve in a cocktail glass.*


Another of Ernest's creations in considerable requisition is **a**

**Special:**                  fresh lemon juice
                              sugar
                              rye
                              dash apricot brandy
                              *Shake well. Serve in a cocktail glass. In the summer, the whole contents of the shaker may be emptied into a Tom Collins glass, filled with soda, and served as a long, refreshing and cooling drink.*


And a cure for butterflies in the stomach is offered by Fred Armour, the house manager:

**Butterflies Cocktail:**     ¼ oz. lemon juice
                              ¼ oz. grenadine
                              ½ oz. applejack
                              ¼ oz. gin
                              shaved ice
                              *Shake well and then strain. Serve in a cocktail glass.*

One of the Club's favorite waiters who is simply known as "Mr. Valentine" supplies the secret of:

**The Swiss Yodeler:**
1 fresh lime
1 tsp. of molasses
½ tsp. of granulated sugar
1½ oz. bacardi rum
*Serve in a chilled cocktail glass.*

Joe Acre, the captain, persuades the customers with a "Palmetto":

**Palmetto Cocktail:**
¼ oz. cointreau
¼ oz. apricot brandy
¼ oz. light rum
¼ oz. lemon juice
*Serve in a cocktail glass.*

The literary touch is supplied by an "Arch of Triumph Cocktail" which is suggested by Lisa Lee, the Stork receptionist, inspired by the capacity for Calvados of the characters in the Remarque novel:

**Arch of Triumph Cocktail:**
⅔ calvados
⅓ lemon juice
1 tsp. sugar
*Stir in cocktail shaker. Shake well and serve in cocktail glass.*

An "Ann Sheridan Cocktail" is the gift of Harry Kaye, the urbane waiter captain of the Cub Room:

**Ann Sheridan Cocktail:**
juice of half lime and leave the skin in mixer
⅓ oz. of orange curaçao
⅔ oz. white bacardi rum
*Shake well and serve in a cocktail glass.*

While a brisk sock from the distaff side is added by Veronica Harrold of the hat checking department:

**Stay Up Late:**
½ oz. lemon juice
½ oz. club soda
2 oz. gin
½ oz. brandy
little sugar
lemon slice
*Serve in a Collins glass.*

Alice Henry, of the Billingsley office staff, offers the "Romance Cocktail"; and the "Victory", both of which originated in Paris during the first world war:

**Romance Cocktail:**
½ oz. brandy (cognac) and curaçao mixed in equal parts
½ oz. Amer-Picon
½ oz. French vermouth
½ oz. Italian vermouth
*Add cracked ice and shake. Serve in a cocktail glass.*

**Victory:**
½ oz. orange and lemon juice mixed in equal parts with several dashes of grenadine
1 oz. French vermouth
1 oz. Italian vermouth
*Add cracked ice and shake. Serve in a cocktail glass.*

The "Pink Top" is the creation of Mario Bellettini, a captain:

**Pink Top:**   1½ oz. gin
                ¾ oz. grand marnier
                ¼ oz. lemon juice
                dash grenadine
                *Shake well and serve very cold.*


While at the end of the procession comes the contribution of Kittie Kincaid of the hat room:

**Whiskey Sour on the Sweet Side:**
                1 oz. rye
                ½ oz. lemon juice
                *Serve with cherry, orange and sugar.*


And Albert Butrice's "Round Robin" from behind the bar:

**Round Robin:**   white of one egg
                   tsp. of sugar
                   1 oz. absinthe
                   1 oz. brandy
                   *Shake well. Serve in a still wine glass.*


And finally Tony Malinary's "Ranger Cocktail":

**Ranger Cocktail:**   ⅓ oz. rum (light)
                       ⅓ oz. gin
                       ⅓ oz. lemon juice
                       sugar to sweeten
                       *Shake well. Serve in cocktail glass.*

# Index by Alphabet:

# Index by Ingredients:

CPSIA information can be obtained
at www.ICGtesting.com
Printed in the USA
BVOW06s0030061217
501667BV00041B/329/P